Christian Science

Christian Science

by
ANTHONY A. HOEKEMA

WILLIAM B. EERDMANS PUBLISHING COMPANY
Grand Rapids, Michigan

The material in this book is an updating of
material originally appearing in *The Four
Major Cults*, Fourth printing, August 1972.

Contents

Preface

The discussion of Christian Science found in this book is organized as follows: First, a brief history of the movement is given, including the main facts about the life of Mary Baker Eddy, followed by a brief account of the Christian Science Church; organization, description of a typical service, membership figures, and geographical distribution. Next the source of authority appealed to by Christian Scientists is taken up. Then, after a description of Christian Science's four basic denials, the doctrines taught by the Christian Science Church are expounded in the order of the customary divisions of Christian theology: God, man, Christ, salvation, the church, the last things.

In setting forth the doctrinal views of the Christian Science Church, I have used primary source material exclusively: the writings of Mary Baker Eddy, particularly *Science and Health*. References to the sources used are given in the footnotes. A bibliography lists all of Mrs. Eddy's major writings, biographies of Mrs. Eddy, histories of Christian Science, and a number of general works. All Scripture quotations not otherwise identified are from the American Standard Version.

Readers of this book are referred to the author's *Four Major Cults* (Eerdmans, 1963) for additional material on the cults. Besides dealing with the doctrinal teachings of Jehovah's Witnesses, Mormonism, and Seventh-day Adventism, *The Four Major Cults* also includes chapters on the challenge of the cults, the distinctive traits of the cult, and the approach to the cultist.

May the Lord use this book for the advancement of His kingdom and for the glory of His name. May He particularly use it to lead many from the errors of Christian Science to the truth as it is in Christ.

Anthony A. Hoekema

Grand Rapids, Michigan
July, 1972

I. History

LIFE OF MARY BAKER EDDY

MARY BAKER EDDY WAS BORN AT BOW, NEW HAMPSHIRE, ON JULY 16, 1821, as the youngest of six children.[1] Her parents were devoutly religious. Her father, Mark Baker, was a stern Calvinist. Mary often disagreed with her father, particularly on such points as the final judgment day, the peril of endless punishment, and the view that God has no mercy toward unbelievers. Mary was a nervous child and missed much schooling as a result. She got her education mostly through her own efforts and through the help of her brothers and sisters, particularly her brother Albert who taught her advanced subjects during summer vacations.

For years Mary was a semi-invalid. One author states that she was afflicted with a spinal weakness which caused spasmodic seizures, followed by prostration which amounted to a complete nervous collapse.[2]

At the age of 17 Mary joined the Congregational Church at Tilton, New Hampshire. In her autobiography, written when she was seventy, she asserts that she refused to accept the somewhat morbid theology of this church. Despite this refusal, however, so she claims, she was accepted into membership.

In 1843 she was married to George Glover. This was a happy marriage but a short-lived one, lasting only a little longer than

---

[1] For this brief biographical sketch I am particularly indebted to Charles S. Braden, *Christian Science Today* (Dallas: Southern Methodist University Press, 1958), pp. 11-41.
[2] Harry S. Goodykoontz, "The Healing Sects," in *The Church Faces the isms*, ed. A. B. Rhodes (New York: Abingdon, 1958), p. 197.

9

half a year. Glover died, leaving her with an unborn child in Charleston, South Carolina, where they were living at the time. Mary went back north and, in September of 1844, gave birth to a son whom she named George. The trip from the South was very hard on her; it appears that from this time on she was never entirely free from pain. It is therefore not surprising that she became preoccupied with the question of health.

In 1853 Mary married dentist Daniel Patterson. This marriage was a very unhappy one. Patterson was not a good provider; he often spent much time practicing in other towns, and was reputed to have become interested in other women. This marriage lasted until 1866, when he and Mary were permanently separated. Seven years later Mary obtained a divorce on the grounds of desertion, though her own later references to this divorce make it appear that Patterson had been guilty of adultery.

During this time her health was still poor. When reports spread through the country that in Portland, Maine, a man named Phineas P. Quimby was effecting remarkable cures without medicine, Mary decided to go to him. She first saw Quimby in 1862; she believed herself to have been healed by him. For a considerable time she was an enthusiastic follower of Quimby, accepting his conviction that he had rediscovered Jesus' own healing methods. Mary tried to follow Quimby's methods, not only with regard to her own health, but also in the treatment of others. She even delivered a public lecture on Quimby's "Spiritual Science Healing Disease."

One of the most heated controversies regarding Mrs. Eddy concerns the relation between her teachings and those of Phineas P. Quimby. Mrs. Eddy herself (who at this time, it will be recalled, was Mrs. Patterson) at first praised Quimby to the skies. Later on, however, she repudiated any indebtedness to him, affirming that he had really borrowed most of his ideas from her, and that actually he had had an impeding effect upon her own teachings. Most non-Christian-Scientists, however, believe that she was greatly indebted to Quimby for her ideas, many writers asserting that she even copied large sections from Quimby's manuscripts, later incorporating this material into *Science and Health*. The "official" Christian Science view is that Quimby was a "mesmerist" healer, and that Mrs. Patterson gave him some of his best ideas. Sibyl Wilbur, the "official" biographer of Mary Baker Eddy, questions the existence of any original Quimby manuscripts.[3] On the other hand, opponents of Christian Science, including George A. Quimby, Phineas's son, maintain that there were manuscripts written by Phineas Quimby, and that Mrs. Patterson made liberal use of them. In fact, in 1921 Horatio W. Dresser published a book edited by him, entitled *The Quimby Manuscripts*, which contained correspondence between Mr. Phineas Quimby and his patients, and also the Quimby manuscripts whose existence had been questioned.[4] People have found a great many parallels between Quimby's writings and Mrs. Eddy's *Science and Health*. Note, for example, the following statement: "We may say at once that, as far as the thought is concerned, *Science and Health* is practically all Quimby."[5]

It will be rather obvious to any unbiased observer that Mrs. Eddy owed many of her ideas to Phineas Quimby. Quimby spoke of his system as "the Science of the Christ"; Mrs. Eddy called her system *Christian Science*.[6] Mrs. Eddy certainly got from Quimby her emphasis on healing by opposing "truth to error." It must also be admitted, of course, that Mrs. Eddy went considerably beyond Quimby. The latter had no intention of founding a separate religious movement.[7]

[3] *The Life of Mary Baker Eddy* (New York: Concord, 1908), p. 104, 105.

[4] Originally published by T. Y. Crowell, N.Y., in 1921, and reprinted in 1961 by the Julian Press, N.Y.

[5] Ernest Sutherland Bates and John V. Dittemore, *Mary Baker Eddy: The Truth and the Tradition* (New York: Knopf, 1932), p. 156.

[6] Walter R. Martin and Norman H. Klann, *The Christian Science Myth* (Grand Rapids: Zondervan, 1955), p. 14. The authors add in a footnote that Quimby even called his system *Christian Science* some years before Mrs. Eddy adopted the name, referring to p. 388 of the *Quimby Manuscripts*. Bates and Dittemore give the exact quotation from Quimby containing the words "Christian Science," and the date when these words were written: Feb., 1863 (*op. cit.*, p. 157, n. 6).

[7] It should be added here that, according to Christian Scientists, what Mrs. Eddy may have borrowed from Quimby was of superficial value, since her system of religious thought is, in their judgment, basically different from this. See Clifford P. Smith, *Historical Sketches* (Boston: Christian Science Publishing Society, 1941), pp. 45-53. Note also the following statement, from DeWitt John's *Christian Science Way of Life* (Englewood Cliffs: Prentice-Hall, 1962): "To be sure, there are certain superficial resemblances between Christian Science and Quimbyism in certain limited directions (e.g., that there is no intelligence in matter) and also an occasional similarity of terminology (e.g., that sickness is 'error' or 'belief'). But the meaning of the terms is radically different in Christian Science" (p. 152).

Phineas Quimby died in January of 1866. On February 1 of that year Mrs. Patterson fell on an icy pavement and was painfully injured. Many years later she told the following version of this fall: this injury, she said, had been pronounced fatal by the physicians. On the third day after her fall, however, she opened her Bible to Matthew 9:2-8 (the story of the healing of the paralytic, including Jesus' words: "Arise, take up thy bed, and go to thy house"). As she read, the healing truth dawned upon her senses; hence she now arose, dressed herself, and was ever afterward in better health than she had enjoyed before.[8] At another time she described Christian Science as a discovery made in February of 1866.[9]

There is some question, however, as to the accuracy of Mrs. Eddy's recollections about this incident. The doctor who attended her at the time, Dr. Alvin M. Cushing of Springfield, Massachusetts, made an affidavit on August 13, 1904, in which he made the following statement:

> I did not at any time declare, or believe, that there was no hope of Mrs. Patterson's recovery, or that she was in a critical condition, and did not at any time say, or believe that she had but three or any other limited number of days to live; and Mrs. Patterson did not suggest, or say, or pretend, or in any way whatever intimate, that on the third day or any other day, of her said illness, she had miraculously recovered or been healed, or that discovering or perceiving the truth or the power employed by Christ to heal the sick, she had, by it, been restored to health.[10]

Further, on February 14, 1866 (hence 13 days after the fall and 10 days after the alleged cure), Mrs. Patterson sent a letter to Julius Dresser, a former pupil of Phineas Quimby, asking him to come and help her since, so she said, "I am slowly failing."[11] It seems

---

[8] Mary Baker Eddy, *Miscellaneous Writings* (Boston, 1896), p. 24. See also *Retrospection and Introspection*, p. 24.

[9] Mary Baker Eddy, *Science and Health with Key to the Scriptures* (Boston, 1934), p. 107.

[10] Bates and Dittemore, *op. cit.*, p. 112. This volume contains the entire text of the affidavit. Dr. Cushing explained that these statements were based upon his own detailed medical records.

[11] The text of the letter is found on p. 109 of Bates and Dittemore's biography. Interestingly enough, though Mrs. Patterson had told Dresser that she was not placing her intelligence in matter, the latter countered, in his reply to her, "If you believe you are failing, then your intelligence is placed in matter" (*ibid.*, p. 110).

quite evident that Mrs. Eddy's memory regarding this incident did not serve her very well.

This event was, however, a turning-point in her life. She now determined to devote her life to emphasizing the healing element of religion. During the next few years Mrs. Patterson (who after her separation from Patterson in 1866 resumed the name of Glover) carried on a growing healing practice, taught others her ideas, and even began to set them down in writing. In 1870, in Lynn, Massachusetts, Mrs. Glover was teaching pupils her system of healing, charging a fee of $300 for a dozen lessons. Though this fee seems high, it must be remembered that, after taking these lessons, one could set himself up as a doctor and charge fees comparable to those of the regular medical practitioners of the day.

In 1875 Mrs. Glover bought a house of her own in Lynn. Also during this year she finished the writing of *Science and Health,* the textbook of Christian Science. Three of her associates helped her get the manuscript into print, since no commercial firm was willing to undertake its publication. Copies of this rare first edition of 1875 are now almost priceless. Also in 1875 the first organization of a society was effected. A small group agreed to contribute regularly in order to rent a public hall; they also employed Mrs. Glover to preach for them on Sundays.

Two years later, in 1877, Mrs. Glover married Asa Gilbert Eddy, a sewing machine agent. Eddy had been the first student of Mrs. Glover to assume the title of "Christian Science Practitioner."

On August 23, 1879, *The Church of Christ (Scientist)* was incorporated and was given a charter; hence we may recognize this date as the official beginning of the Christian Science Church. The headquarters of this church were to be in Boston; the purpose of the incorporation was "to transact the business necessary to the worship of God."[12] The Christian Science *Church Manual* states, however, that the purpose of the church was to be: "to commemorate the word and works of our Master, which should reinstate primitive Christianity and its lost element of healing."[13] Mrs. Eddy was appointed on the committee which was to draft the tenets of the Mother Church; after the charter had been obtained,

12 Edwin F. Dakin, *Mrs. Eddy* (New York: Scribner, 1930), p. 151.
13 P. 17. The edition used is the 89th, copyrighted in 1936.

Mrs. Eddy was extended a call to become the pastor of the church.[14]

In 1881 Mrs. Eddy founded the "Massachusetts Metaphysical College" in her home at Lynn. Later she moved this institution to Boston and continued to instruct students there. During these years Mrs. Eddy continued to revise her book and to write other books and magazine articles.

It should be noted here that a retired Unitarian minister by the name of James Henry Wiggin was "literary adviser" to Mrs. Eddy from 1885 to 1891. Bates and Dittemore quote from an article in the *New York World* of November 6, 1906, written six years after Wiggin's death, by Livingston Wright, the former's literary executor, which contains an account of what Wiggin had told Wright about his relationship to Mrs. Eddy. Dakin also quotes from this article, much of which was written in the first person. Wiggin is here quoted as describing how Mrs. Eddy came to him with a manuscript of *Science and Health,* asking him to put it into better literary shape. She did not give him the impression that any major revision was necessary, but that there were "doubtless a few things here and there, that would require the assistance of a fresh mind."[15] Wiggin's reaction to the manuscript, as reported in the article, was as follows:

> Of all the dissertations a literary helper ever inspected, I do not believe one ever saw a treatise to surpass this. The misspelling, capitalization and punctuation were dreadful, but these were not the things that feazed me. It was the thought and the general elemental arrangement of the work. There were passages that flatly and absolutely contradicted things that had preceded, and scattered all through were incorrect references to historical and philosophical matters.
>
> . . . I was convinced that the only way in which I could undertake the requested revision would be to begin absolutely at the first page and rewrite the whole thing![16]

Wiggin further indicated, according to the *New York World* article, that he had to rewrite practically every sentence. He found that Mrs. Eddy knew absolutely nothing of the ancient languages, and that her English was so poor that he virtually had to revise the

---

[14] Note how completely Mrs. Eddy dominated this church from the very beginning.

[15] Dakin, *op. cit.,* p. 225.

[16] *Ibid.* Cf. Bates and Dittemore, *op. cit.,* p. 267.

work *in toto*.[17] It would seem, therefore, that Mrs. Eddy was not only indebted to Quimby for many of her ideas, but that she likewise owed a considerable debt to Wiggin for having put her thoughts into readable English, and for having corrected many of her references.

During these years Mrs. Eddy was also engrossed in problems of organization and administration; she had to make occasional trips to court to defend her interests. Under the stress of these responsibilities, ill health once more overtook her. She now began to attribute her illnesses to the evil influences of her enemies, describing these influences as forms of "malicious animal magnetism."[18] Because her teeth had to be extracted, she resorted to artificial dentures; she also began to wear glasses;[19] and, when her pain would not yield to purely metaphysical healing methods, she used to call in a doctor to administer morphine.[20] She justified her usage of these non-mental measures by various types of arguments. As an example, note the following from *Science and Health*:

> If from an injury or from any cause, a Christian Scientist were seized with pain so violent that he could not treat himself mentally — and the Scientists had failed to relieve him, — the sufferer could call a surgeon who would give him a hypodermic

---

[17] In reply, however, Christian Scientists state that the *New York World* article is not reliable, since the words attributed by it to Wiggin were actually Wright's own reconstructions of what Wiggin was reputed to have said to him some seven years earlier (Robert Peel, *Christian Science: Its Encounter with American Culture* [New York: Henry Holt, 1958], p. 118, n. 24). They also cite Mrs. Eddy's own statement about her indebtedness to Wiggin in *Miscellany*, pp. 317-18, where she claims that she only employed him to improve her grammar and to remove ambiguities from her writing. It seems difficult to determine exactly how much Mrs. Eddy owed to Wiggin.

[18] Or M. A. M. for short. The expression "animal magnetism" was coined by Friedrich Anton Mesmer (1733-1815), an Austrian physician, to describe the hypnotic influence he had on his patients. Mrs. Eddy added the adjective "malicious." It may be noted that the ascription of personal afflictions to the influence of enemies is a trait typical of paranoid personalities, and has affinities with the delusions of persecution which are so common in these personalities.

[19] Peel, however (*op. cit.*, p. 95), asserts that she was healed of this eye affliction in later years.

[20] Bates and Dittemore give evidence for the fact that Mrs. Eddy was addicted to morphine during part of her life, and that during most of her life she had to battle against "the morphine habit" (*op. cit.*, pp. 41-42, 151, 445).

injection, then, when the belief of pain was lulled, he could handle his own case mentally.[21]

In 1882 Mrs. Eddy's third husband, Asa Gilbert Eddy, died from organic heart disease. Mrs. Eddy, however, announced to the newspapers that he had been murdered with arsenic mentally administered by "certain parties here in Boston who had sworn to injure" the Eddys.[22]

In 1886 the National Christian Scientists' Association was organized, indicating that the movement was becoming national in scope. In 1889 Mrs. Eddy retired from the local leadership in Boston and moved to Concord, New Hampshire. In 1892 she organized the Mother Church in Boston, calling it *The First Church of Christ, Scientist*. In her retirement at Concord she continued to revise *Science and Health* and to write extensively. In 1908 she founded the *Christian Science Monitor*, a daily which is still being published, stressing the edifying instead of the seamy side of the news. The *Monitor* is, in fact, one of the outstanding newspapers in the world, noted for the excellence of its reporting and the wide range of its coverage.

There were troubles toward the end of her life. Augusta Stetson, head of the New York church, was banished from the church she had built because her growing popularity began to threaten Mrs. Eddy's supremacy. After some of Mrs. Eddy's pupils had begun to believe that, if one became sufficiently spiritual, it would be possible to conceive a child without the help of a man, one of these disciples, Mrs. Josephine Woodbury, claimed that a child born to her in 1890 had been virginally conceived. This claim — which, needless to say, was played up by the newspapers — so embarrassed Mrs. Eddy that she eventually had Mrs. Woodbury excommunicated. When, after this excommunication, the child in question, who had been named "the Prince of Peace," tried to attend the Christian Science Sunday school, he was "lifted up by his coat-collar and bodily thrown out"![23]

On December 3, 1910, Mrs. Eddy, who had taught that there is no death, quietly "passed on." Dakin relates the following conversation which took place shortly before her death between

---

[21] P. 464. Note the interesting suggestion that a hypodermic injection can lull "the belief of pain."

[22] From an article in the Boston *Daily Globe* of June 4, 1882, quoted by Bates and Dittemore, *op. cit.*, p. 219.

[23] Bates and Dittemore, *op. cit.*, p. 364-67.

Mrs. Eddy and one of her closest associates, Adam Dickey: "If I should ever leave here, will you promise me that you will say that I was mentally murdered?" "Yes, Mother."[24]

THE CHRISTIAN SCIENCE CHURCH

Since Mrs. Eddy's death, control of the Christian Science denomination has been vested in a self-perpetuating Board of Directors, the first members of which had been appointed by Mrs. Eddy herself. The rules whereby the church is governed, plus a number of by-laws, are found in the *Church Manual,* written by Mrs. Eddy. Mrs. Eddy had incorporated into the *Church Manual* the stipulation that with respect to these rules nothing could be adopted, amended, or annulled without the written consent of the Leader.[25] Thus her control as long as she lived was complete, and, since she cannot now give written consent to any change, it is impossible to alter the rules of the church in any way today. The Christian Science Church is therefore a highly authoritarian organization. There have been a number of individuals within the denomination who have resented this authoritarian control and have pleaded for greater liberty, both in the areas of church government and teaching; they, however, have either stepped out of the church voluntarily or have been forced out.

Though at first Mrs. Eddy used to preach at the services, in 1895 she promulgated a by-law which "ordained the Bible and *Science and Health* as pastor on this planet of all the churches of the Christian Science denomination."[26] This means that at the present time no sermon is preached in Christian Science services. Prescribed portions of Scripture are read by the Second Reader; these are followed by the reading of correlative passages from *Science and Health* by the First Reader. The same lesson is read on a particular Sunday in every Christian Science Church the world around. Some Christian Science hymns are sung, and there is usually a selection by a soloist. There is also a period of silent prayer and the audible repetition of the Lord's Prayer — the latter, however, is followed by a quotation from *Science and Health*

---

[24] *Op. cit.,* pp. 504-505. Dakin is quoting from Dickey's *Memoirs of Mary Baker Eddy.*
[25] Article 35, Sec. 3, of the 89th edition (p. 105).
[26] Charles S. Braden, *These Also Believe* (New York: Macmillan, 1960), p. 196. This rule, in modified form, is found in Article 14, Sec. 1, of the *Church Manual* (p. 58).

(pp. 16 and 17), giving Mrs. Eddy's interpretation of the "spiritual sense" of this prayer.

A Board of Lectureship has been set up; each church is expected to call for a lecturer at least once a year. Lecturers must send copies of their lectures to the clerk of the Mother Church before delivery. A Committee on Publication functions for the Mother Church in each state and in Canada for the purpose of correcting false or misleading statements in the public press concerning Christian Science or its founder. Christian Scientists are not permitted to buy from publishers or bookstores who have on sale "obnoxious books" — meaning books which are unfavorable to Christian Science. At times the church has attempted to suppress the sale of books which are unfavorable to it or to its founder. Every branch church is expected to maintain a reading room where one may read, buy, or borrow authorized Christian Science literature. The closest equivalents to the ordained pastors of Protestantism in the Christian Science Church are the practitioners: people who have received instruction in Christian Science and who devote their full time to the practice of its healing methods. Wednesday evening meetings at Christian Science churches are "testimony meetings," at which people testify about their healings.

The Christian Science Church has not experienced as rapid a growth as have the Mormons, the Seventh-day Adventists, or the Jehovah's Witnesses. One of the difficulties we encounter in attempting to assess the size of the Christian Science Church is that a provision of the Church Manual prohibits the numbering of members for publication. Christian Scientists are not averse, however, to publishing statistics about the number of their churches. In a letter dated June 28, 1972, from Mr. J. Buroughs Stokes, Manager of the Committees on Publication of the Christian Science Church, it was stated that there were at that time "upward of 3,200 churches in our denomination." Christian Science churches may vary in size all the way from perhaps 1500 members in the larger cities to 50 members or less in the smaller towns. It will be noted that this number of churches is considerably less than the 16,726 churches listed in the Seventh-day Adventist Statistical Report for the year ending December 31, 1971; or the 27,154 congregations listed by Jehovah's Witnesses in the January 1, 1972, issue of the *Watchtower*. Though it is difficult to know exactly what these figures mean in terms of total membership, it seems quite obvious that the Christian Science

Church has not grown as rapidly as have the Seventh-day Adventists or the Jehovah's Witnesses.

The total number of Christian Science practitioners at the present time, according to the above-mentioned letter, is approximately 5,700, of whom about 1,160 are outside the United States. The *Christian Science Journal* of 1931 listed 10,177 practitioners, whereas the 1958 *Journal* listed 9,567.[27] It is clear, therefore, that the number of practitioners has been steadily declining since 1931. During this same period, however, the number of churches increased from 2,466 in 1931[28] to "upward of 3,200" in 1972.

The geographical distribution of Christian Scientists resembles that of the Mormons in at least one respect: most of the members of both of these groups are found within the United States. According to the above-mentioned letter from Mr. Stokes, 775 Christian Science churches are to be found outside the United States. This is a ratio of about one-fourth the total number. If Christian Science churches outside the United States are of approximately the same size as those inside, it would seem that out of every four Christian Scientists in the world, about three would be found in the United States.

The various churches and societies are listed according to geographical distribution on the pages of the *Christian Science Journal*. Societies are groups of Christian Scientists not large enough or strong enough to be organized as churches. From the July, 1972, issue of the *Christian Science Journal* we learn that the foreign country which has the largest number of Christian Science churches is Great Britain (including England, Scotland, Ireland, and Wales). Next come West Germany, Canada, and the combined countries of Australia and New Zealand — each of these, however, has only about one-fourth as many churches as has Great Britain. Smaller numbers of Christian Science churches and societies are found in Africa, Asia, South America, and in such European countries as the Netherlands, Switzerland, and France. It appears quite evident that most Christian Scientists are found in English-speaking countries. It is interesting to note that in the United States the largest number of Christian Science churches and societies in any state is to be found in California, Los Angeles alone having 46 churches.

The following information was also gleaned from the Stokes letter: Christian Scientists have one central publishing house, the Christian

---

[27] Braden, *Christian Science Today*, p. 271.
[28] *Ibid.*, the figure having been obtained from the 1931 *Christian Science Journal*.

Science Publishing Society in Boston. Their daily newspaper, *The Christian Science Monitor*, is printed in five cities (four in the United States, and also in London, England); it has a circulation of more than 215,000. Christian Scientists also publish the following major periodicals: *The Christian Science Journal,* published monthly; *The Christian Science Sentinel*, published weekly; *The Herald of Christian Science*, published monthly and quarterly in 12 foreign languages as well as in English Braille; and *The Christian Science Quarterly*, containing the Bible lessons studied daily by Christian Scientists. Religious publications include *The Christian Science Hymnal*, as well as other books and pamphlets. Mrs. Eddy's *Science and Health* is now being published in 12 languages other than English. Various other materials appear in 17 languages other than English.

Christian Scientists maintain a weekly nationwide radio program, *The Truth that Heals*, which is also broadcast outside the United States.

Two sanatoriums, one on the East Coast and one on the West Coast, are maintained by the Mother Church for those relying solely on Christian Science treatment. The church also maintains a home for elderly Christian Scientists who have faithfully served the denomination over a period of years. In addition, there is an independently owned and operated sanatorium for those with mental difficulties who are relying on Christian Science for healing. Institutional work in prisons, reformatories, and mental hospitals is carried on by the Mother Church locally, and by the branch churches throughout the country.

II. Source of Authority

We begin our discussion of the doctrinal tenets of this group with the question which is of basic importance: What is the source of authority? Christian Science ostensibly claims to accept the Bible as its final source of authority. On page 497 of *Science and Health* a brief statement of the "important points, or religious tenets" of Christian Science is given. The first of these reads as follows: "As adherents of Truth, we take the inspired Word of the Bible as our sufficient guide to eternal Life." To the same effect are the following affirmations of Mrs. Eddy:

> The Bible has been my only authority. I have had no other guide in "the straight and narrow way" of Truth.[29]
> In following these leadings of scientific revelation, the Bible was my only textbook.[30]

At first hearing, these statements make it appear as if Christian Scientists do not differ from Protestant Christians in acknowledging the Scriptures as their final authority in matters of faith and life. In actual practice, however, Christian Scientists accept the Bible only as interpreted by Mrs. Eddy, whose book, *Science and Health, with Key to the Scriptures,* is really their ultimate source of authority, and is thus placed above the Bible. In proof of this assertion, I advance the following considerations:

(1) *Mrs. Eddy is believed by Christian Scientists to have received her insights through divine revelation.* Christian Scientists accept as gospel truth the following assertion by Mrs. Eddy: "No human pen nor tongue taught me the Science contained in this

[29] *Science and Health*, p. 126.
[30] *Ibid.*, p. 110.

book, *Science and Health. . . ."*[31] The obvious implication is that
she was taught her views by a superhuman source: namely, by
God Himself. This conclusion is confirmed by the following
statement:

> In the year 1866, I discovered the Christ Science or divine
> laws of Life, Truth, and Love, and named my discovery Chris-
> tian Science. God had been graciously preparing me during
> many years for the reception of this final revelation of the ab-
> solute divine Principle of scientific mental healing.[32]

Above this paragraph Mrs. Eddy placed the following Scriptural
quotation: "But I certify you, brethren, that the gospel which
was preached of me is not after man. For I neither received it
of man, neither was I taught it, but by the revelation of Jesus
Christ." At another place Mrs. Eddy maintained that, in writing
Science and Health, she was only "echoing the harmonies of
heaven":

> I should blush to write of "Science and Health with Key to
> the Scriptures" as I have, were it of human origin, and were I,
> apart from God, its author. But, as I was only a scribe echo-
> ing the harmonies of heaven in divine metaphysics, I cannot
> be super-modest in my estimate of the Christian Science text-
> book.[33]

We note thus at the outset the claim, common to all cults, that the
group in question has access to a source of direct divine revelation.
   (2) *Mrs. Eddy's book,* Science and Health, *is recognized by
Christian Scientists as their final authority.* For proof I quote
from *Science and Health*:

> A Christian Scientist requires my work *Science and Health*
> for his textbook, and so do all his students and patients. Why?
> *First:* Because it is the voice of Truth to this age, and contains
> the full statement of Christian Science, or the Science of heal-
> ing through Mind. *Second:* Because it was the first book known,
> containing a thorough statement of Christian Science. Hence
> it gave the first rules for demonstrating this Science, and reg-
> istered the revealed Truth uncontaminated by human hypoth-
> eses.[34]

---

[31] *Ibid.*
[32] *Ibid.,* p. 107. Note particularly the expression, *this final revelation.*
[33] *The First Church of Christ, Scientist, and Miscellany* (Boston, 1941),
p. 115.
[34] *Ibid.,* pp. 456-57.

Note that *Science and Health* is here said to be the *voice of Truth* and to be *uncontaminated by human hypotheses.* Since Christian Scientists accept *Science and Health* as true, they must also accept as true this estimate of the book — an estimate which raises it far above every other book, including the Bible.

Small wonder, therefore, that Charles S. Braden asserts:

> *Science and Health with Key to the Scriptures* is a second scripture to the Christian Scientists. This is seen in the constant use made of it, and the authority that is accorded it, equal to or greater than the Bible itself, since the true meaning of the latter is known only through the interpretation given it in *Science and Health.*[35]

The very fact that Christian Scientists have this book read publicly alongside of the Bible in their Sunday services substantiates Dr. Braden's affirmation.

(3) *The Bible is often said to be in error.* Note first the following significant statement:

> The decisions by vote of Church Councils as to what should and should not be considered Holy Writ; the manifest mistakes in the ancient versions; the thirty thousand different readings in the Old Testament, and the three hundred thousand in the New, — these facts show how a mortal and material sense stole into the divine record, with its own hue darkening to some extent the inspired pages.[36]

Contrast with this the assertion on page 99 of *Science and Health*: "Christian Science is unerring and divine. . . ," and the previously quoted claim that *Science and Health* is uncontaminated by human hypotheses. As Mormons contend that the Bible is full or errors whereas the *Book of Mormon* is errorless (see above, pp. 18-19), so Christian Scientists allege that the Bible has many errors, but that they have a source of authority which is not subject to these human frailties. It is becoming increasingly clear that there is much which various cults have in common!

Let us look at some examples of these supposed errors in Scripture. Christian Scientists believe that the second chapter of Gen-

---

[35] *These Also Believe*, p. 209.
[36] *Science and Health*, p. 139. Note the vagueness of this assertion. We are not told which of the ancient versions had "manifest mistakes," nor of what sort they were. Neither are we given any samples of these variant readings, most of which, as anyone conversant with the facts knows, do not affect the meaning of the passage in question to the slightest degree.

esis is grossly in error. Taking a leaf from higher criticism, Mrs.
Eddy contended that two distinct documents had been used in
the writing of the early part of the Book of Genesis: the Elohistic
and the Jehovistic.[37] Genesis 1, representing the Elohistic document, describes man as having been created in the image of God;
this account of creation is "spiritual" and true. Genesis 2, however, derived from the inferior Jehovistic document, represents
man as formed of the dust of the ground; this account of creation
is false and in error:

> The Science and truth of the divine creation have been pre-
> sented in the verses already considered [those of Genesis 1], and
> now the opposite error, a material view of creation, is to be set
> forth. The second chapter of Genesis contains a statement of
> this material view of God and the universe, a statement which
> is the exact opposite of scientific truth as before recorded.[38]
> The Science of the first record proves the falsity of the second.
> If one is true, the other is false, for they are antagonistic.[39]
> Is this addition to His creation [Gen. 2:7] real or unreal? Is
> it the truth, or is it a lie concerning man and God?
> It must be a lie, for God presently curses the ground.[40]

Error, furthermore, is not limited to the Old Testament. In another book Mrs. Eddy says:

> To suppose that Jesus did actually anoint the blind man's eyes
> with his spittle, is as absurd as to think, according to the report
> of some, that Christian Scientists sit in back-to-back seances
> with their patients, for the divine power to filter from vertebrae
> to vertebrae.[41]

(4) *The historical contents of the Bible are said to be unim-
portant.* Listen to this astounding statement, taken from a report
made of one of Mrs. Eddy's sermons: "The material record of
the Bible, she said, is no more important to our well-being than
the history of Europe and America; but the spiritual application
bears upon our eternal life."[42] What is being said here is that the
life, death, and resurrection of Jesus Christ, as historical events,
are no more important for our spiritual well-being than, say, the
defeat of Napoleon by Wellington or the discovery of America

[37] *Ibid.,* p. 523.
[38] *Ibid.,* p. 521.
[39] *Ibid.,* p. 522.
[40] *Ibid.,* p. 524. One wonders, however, where this "lie" came from,
and how it came to appear in a book which is supposed to be the
"sufficient guide to eternal life," and the "only authority"!
[41] *Miscellaneous Writings* (Boston, 1896), p. 171.
[42] *Ibid.,* p. 170.

by Columbus! Yet no less an authority than the Apostle Paul exclaims: "If Christ hath not been raised, your faith is vain; ye are yet in your sins" (I Cor. 15:17).

(5) *Christian Scientists so completely reinterpret the Bible as to read into it any meaning they wish.* The key to their method of Bible interpretation is found in the following statement of Mrs. Eddy: "The literal rendering of the Scriptures makes them nothing valuable, but often is the foundation of unbelief and hopelessness. The metaphysical rendering is health and peace and hope for all."[43]

Let us note a few examples of these "metaphysical renderings." After citing Genesis 1:1, Mrs. Eddy explains: "This creation consists of the unfolding of spiritual ideas and their identities, which are embraced in the infinite Mind and forever reflected."[44] On Genesis 1:6 ("And God said, Let there be a firmament. . ."), Mrs. Eddy comments as follows: "Spiritual understanding, by which human conception, material sense, is separated from Truth, is the firmament."[45] Genesis 1:9, which reads, "And God said, Let the waters under the heavens be gathered together unto one place. . . ," is "officially" interpreted as follows: "Spirit, God, gathers unformed thoughts into their proper channels, and unfolds these thoughts, even as he opens the petals of a holy purpose in order that the purpose may appear."[46] When one pages through the Glossary found on pages 579-599 of *Science and Health,* he is regaled by twenty pages of comparable feats of exegetical acrobatics. It need hardly be added that by means of this method one can read into Scripture the most fantastic ideas the human mind can concoct. One may admire the ingenuity with which these interpretations are fabricated, but can one call this *listening to Scripture?*

We conclude that the Bible is decidedly not Christian Science's "only authority," but that the writings of Mrs. Eddy, particularly *Science and Health,* are for Christian Science what the writings of Joseph Smith are for Mormonism and the works of Ellen G. White are for Seventh-day Adventism. In other words, in Christian Science as well as in these other cults, the opinions of the cult leader are elevated above the Bible and are recognized as the supreme source of authority.

43 *Ibid.,* p. 169.
44 *Science and Health,* pp. 502-503.
45 *Ibid.,* p. 505.
46 *Ibid.,* p. 506.

III. Doctrines

BASIC DENIALS

On page 27 of *Miscellaneous Writings,* Mrs. Eddy makes the following statement: "Here also is found the pith of the basal statement, the cardinal point in Christian Science, that matter and evil (including all inharmony, sin, disease, death) are *unreal.*" Let us look at these "unrealities" briefly, and see what Christian Science teaches about them. There are four of them: matter, evil, disease, and death.

MATTER

Mrs. Eddy says:

> My first plank in the platform of Christian Science is as follows: "There is no life, truth, intelligence, nor substance in matter. All is infinite Mind and its infinite manifestation, for God is All-in-all. Spirit is immortal Truth; matter is mortal error. Spirit is the real and eternal; matter is the unreal and temporal."[47]

Christian Science therefore contends that matter does not really exist. Matter is defined in the Glossary of *Science and Health* as an illusion, as "the opposite of Truth; the opposite of Spirit; the opposite of God; that of which immortal Mind takes no cognizance; that which mortal mind sees, feels, hears, tastes, and smells only in belief" (p. 591). Mortal mind is defined on the same page as "nothing claiming to be something . . . error creating other errors; a suppositional material sense. . . ." Matter, therefore, has no real existence even in the mind; it is an illusion held by an illusion.

[47] *Miscellaneous Writings,* p. 21.

Why is the reality of matter denied? Because matter is the opposite of God, and God is the only real substance (p. 468).[48] When one observes that we learn to know the existence of matter through our senses, Christian Science replies by saying that our senses are deceitful (p. 395), and false; that, in fact, they defraud and lie (p. 489). The corporeal senses, therefore, are "the only source of evil and error" (p. 489).

It apparently never occurred to Mrs. Eddy that by undermining the reliability of the senses she was taking away the foundation for all knowledge, including that taught by Christian Science. If my senses only defraud and lie, the sense of sight with the help of which I read *Science and Health* also defrauds me, and thus I can learn nothing whatever about the truth. Triumphantly Mrs. Eddy explains that astronomical science contradicted the testimony of corporeal sense to the effect that the sun rises and sets while the earth stands still (p. 493); it apparently never occurred to her that Galileo arrived at his new understanding of the workings of the solar system by looking through a telescope with the aid of his corporeal senses!

EVIL AND SIN

For Christian Science evil is nothing (p. 287), unreal (p. 71), an illusion and a false belief (p. 480). Sin, which may in most cases be equated with evil, is a delusion (p. 204), an illusion (p. 494). Note the following statement:

> All reality is in God and His creation. . . . That which He creates is good, and He makes all that is made. Therefore the only reality of sin, sickness, or death is the awful fact that unrealities seem real to human, erring belief, until God strips off their disguise (p. 472).

So there is no such thing as evil or sin.

In answer to the question, "If God made all that was made, and it was good, where did evil originate?" Mrs. Eddy replies: "It never originated or existed as an entity. It is but a false belief."[49]

---

[48] Because most of the quotations and references in the remainder of this chapter will be to *Science and Health,* undesignated page references occurring in this chapter from now on are to this book. Thus (p. 468) following a statement means page 468 in the 1934 ed. of *Science and Health.*

[49] *Miscellaneous Writings,* p. 45. The questioner is bound to ask at this point, But where did the false belief come from? This point is, needless to say, the Achilles' heel of Christian Science. There simply is no explanation in this system for the universal "false belief" that matter exists.

DISEASE

On this question Mrs. Eddy says: "The cause of all so-called disease is mental, a mortal fear, a mistaken belief or conviction of the necessity and power of ill-health. . ." (p. 377). Disease is an illusion and a delusion (p 348). ". . . The evidence of the senses is not to be accepted in the case of sickness, any more than it is in the case of sin" (p. 386). "Man is never sick, for Mind is not sick and matter cannot be" (p. 393).

Consequently, the cure of sickness for Christian Science is to help a person understand that he is not really sick, that his pain is imaginary, and that his imagined disease is only the result of a false belief.

DEATH

Death is defined in the Glossary of *Science and Health* as follows: "An illusion, the lie of life in matter; the unreal and untrue. . ." (p. 584). The definition continues: "Any material evidence of death is false, for it contradicts the spiritual facts of being." Death is only a "belief" which must finally be conquered by eternal Life (p. 380). Note the following sentences:

> If it is true that man lives, this fact can never change in Science to the opposite belief that man dies. . . . Death is but another phase of the dream that existence can be material. . . . The dream of death must be mastered by Mind here or hereafter. . . . Life is real, and death is the illusion (pp. 427-28).

It is rather embarrassing to Christian Scientists to have it pointed out to them that death still does occur in their ranks. Their position would seem to be that, though man has not yet attained to the state in which he can overcome death, such a state may finally be attained.[50] Mrs. Eddy never provided an official ritual for funerals, though she did provide orders of service for other occasions.

It seems quite surprising, too, that Mrs. Eddy herself apparently did not have enough faith to avoid death. Some of her followers did not think that she had died; Mrs. Augusta Stetson, in fact, wrote a letter in which she indignantly rejected newspaper accounts of her death, declaring in italics, "Mary Baker Eddy never died."[51] Others looked hopefully for her resurrection.[52] The officers of the

50 Bates and Dittemore, *op. cit.*, p. 451.
51 James Snowden, *The Truth About Christian Science* (Philadelphia: Westminster, 1920), p. 154, n. 1.
52 Dakin, *op. cit.*, p. 520.

church, however, issued an official statement to the effect that they did not look for Mrs. Eddy's return to this world.[53]

DOCTRINE OF GOD

THE BEING OF GOD

It is very difficult to form a clear idea of God as He is conceived of by Mrs. Eddy. In attempting to define God, she often simply piles up a series of words, without defining any one of them. In brief we may say that, for Mrs. Eddy and Christian Science, whatever is good is God, and whatever is not God does not really exist, though it may seem to exist to erring, mortal mind. God, to the Christian Scientist, is divine Mind, and Mind is all that truly exists.[54]

Mrs. Eddy summarizes her views about God in the following four statements:

1. God is All-in-all.
2. God is good. Good is Mind.
3. God, Spirit, being all, nothing is matter.
4. Life, God, omnipotent good, deny death, evil, sin, disease.
Disease, sin, death, deny good, omnipotent God, Life (p. 113).

God is described on another page as follows: "Divine Principle, Life, Truth, Love, Soul, Spirit, Mind" (p. 115). God is further said to be substance, and the only intelligence of the universe, including man (p. 330). On page 331 we are told that, since God is All-in-all, "nothing possesses reality nor existence except the divine Mind and His ideas."

All this adds up to a pantheism which is thoroughgoing and all-embracing: all is God and God is all. All that truly exists is God and God is Spirit; hence everything that is not spirit does not exist. When the question is asked whether Mrs. Eddy's God is personal, it is difficult to give a clear and unambiguous answer. On the one hand, the descriptions of God so far noted seem to point to an impersonal principle rather than to a personal being. In fact, in one place Mrs. Eddy says, "We must learn that God is infinitely more than a person, or finite form, can contain; that God is a divine *Whole,* and *All,* an all-pervading intelligence and

[53] Bates and Dittemore, *op. cit.,* p. 451.
[54] It is to be observed that whenever words like mind, truth, love, soul, and the like, are capitalized in *Science and Health,* they refer to the deity; whereas when such words are uncapitalized, they do not.

Love, a divine, infinite Principle. . . ."[55]   In *Science and Health,*
however, she affirms, "God is individual and personal in a scientific sense, but not in any anthropomorphic sense" (pp. 336-37).
Again, on another page, she says, "If the term personality, as applied to God, means infinite personality, then God *is* infinite *Person,* — in the sense of infinite personality, but not in the lower
sense" (p. 116).   Braden concludes that Mrs. Eddy "oscillates
continually between the personal and impersonal thought of
God."[56]   Though this may appear so when one compares various
of her statements about God, the basic thrust of her God-concept
is, however, definitely impersonal.   For a God who is not above
His universe but is identified with it as the All cannot be a truly
personal God.   This point will become more evident as we shall
discuss, later in this chapter, the works of God.

Christian Science repudiates the orthodox Trinity.   We read in
Science and Health: "The theory of three persons in one God
(that is, a personal Trinity or Tri-unity) suggests polytheism,
rather than the one ever-present I AM" (p. 256).   Though Mrs.
Eddy thus denied the tri-personality of God, she apparently felt
compelled to make certain concessions to the Trinitarian conception:

> Life, Truth, and Love constitute the triune Person called God,
> — that is, the triply divine Principle, Love.   They represent a
> trinity in unity, three in one, — the same in essence, though
> multiform in office: God the Father-Mother; Christ the spiritual
> idea of sonship; divine Science or the Holy Comforter.[57]   These
> three express in divine Science the threefold, essential nature
> of the infinite (pp. 331-32).

It should be quite evident that Mrs. Eddy's Trinity bears no more
resemblance to the Trinity of the Scriptures than does that of
Georg Wilhelm Hegel, for whom the Trinity was but a pictorial
way of representing the impersonal Absolute, and the movement
of the Absolute from thesis through antithesis to synthesis.

Reference has previously been made to the distinction Mrs.
Eddy makes between the so-called Elohistic and Jehovistic docu-

[55] *Miscellaneous Writings,* p. 16.   Cf. the following statement from
Science and Health: ". . . To reach his [Jesus'] example and to test its
unerring Science . . . a better understanding of God as divine Principle,
Love, rather than personality or the man Jesus, is required" (p. 473).
[56] *These Also Believe,* p. 202.
[57] Note that here Mrs. Eddy equates Christian Science with the third
"person" of the Trinity!

ments presumed to underlie the Book of Genesis (above, p. 24). It is significant to note that this distinction between the names of God is applied by her to two distinct God-concepts. Elohim, so she asserts, is the name of the one Spirit or intelligence who is the true God (p. 591). Jehovah, however, is the name of the God "of limited Hebrew faith";[58] in *Science and Health* she says, "The Jewish tribal Jehovah was a man-projected God, liable to wrath, repentance, and human changeableness" (p. 140). This distinction, however, is completely untenable, since in many passages in the Hebrew Old Testament the two names, Jehovah and Elohim, occur side by side. In blissful ignorance of the fact that the Hebrew of Psalm 23:1 reads, "Jehovah [*Yahweh*] is my shepherd," Mrs. Eddy renders the verse: "Divine love is my shepherd," thus equating the Jewish tribal Jehovah of limited Hebrew faith with Divine love! (p. 578).

THE WORKS OF GOD

Decrees. It is quite obvious that a God who is identified with all that exists cannot be said to foreordain what comes to pass, since he has no existence apart from the universe. Accordingly, we find that Christian Science totally repudiates the Biblical teaching that God has foreordained all that happens, including the faith of His people. In her autobiographical volume, *Retrospection and Introspection,* Mrs. Eddy tells how, while she was in her teens, the doctrine of unconditional election or predestination greatly troubled her. She further relates that her worries about this doctrine made her ill, that her father kept stressing this doctrine and others which she disliked, but that her mother bade her lean on God's love. Soon her fever was gone and, so she continues, "the 'horrible decree' of predestination — as John Calvin rightly called his own tenet — forever lost its power over me."[59]

We are therefore not surprised to find her referring, in *Science and Health,* to "the practically rejected doctrine of the predestina-

[58] *Unity of Good* (Boston, 1936), p. 14.
[59] Pp. 13-14 (Boston, 1920). It should be noted at this point that what Calvin called a "horrible decree" (*decretum horribile*) in *Inst.* III, 23, 7 is not the decree of predestination (which he elsewhere calls a most useful doctrine and one with very sweet fruit, III, 21, 1), but the decree that Adam's fall involved his descendants in eternal death. Calvin insists that this latter decree is by no means the only decree God made.

tion of souls to damnation or salvation" (p. 150). Elsewhere, referring to another teaching which she rejects, she says, "This teaching
is even more pernicious than the old doctrine of foreordination, —
the election of a few to be saved, while the rest are damned. . ."
(p. 38). In another book Mrs. Eddy denies that God either
foreknew or foreordained evil, since evil does not exist.[60]

There is, then, no foreordination or predestination in Christian Science. The following statement, in fact, has universalistic
overtones:

> "Which were born, not of blood, nor of the will of the flesh."
> This passage refers to man's primal, spiritual existence, created
> neither from dust nor carnal desire. . . . The apostle indicates no
> personal plan of a personal Jehovah, partial and finite; but the
> possibility of all finding their place in God's great love, the
> eternal heritage of the Elohim, His sons and daughters.[61]

Creation. Granted the Christian Science view of God, it is
not possible to arrive at a real doctrine of creation. For if there
is no such thing as matter, God cannot have called a material
universe into being. If time is considered equivalent to matter
and error (p. 595), there can be no such thing as a creation in
time. And if all is God, this *all* cannot have been created by
God, since God has no existence apart from the all.

This is precisely what we find as we peruse Christian Science
writings. Matter, as has been seen, does not exist. The existence
of a realm of spiritual beings, ordinarily called angels and demons,
is also denied. Angels, it is said, are simply "God's thoughts
passing to man" (p. 581). The devil, it is said, is "evil; a lie;
error" (p. 584); thus his existence as a personal being is rejected.
Similarly, the existence of demons is denied; Mrs. Eddy speaks
of "the wicked endeavors of suppositional demons,"[62] and in
Pulpit and Press she quotes, apparently with approval, a passage
from a Christian Science sermon which speaks of "the demons
of evil thought."[63]

If there is no material universe, and if there are no angels
or demons, what is left to form a possible object for creation?

[60] *Unity of Good,* p. 19.
[61] *Miscellaneous Writings,* p. 182.
[62] *Ibid.,* p. 19.
[63] P. 29 (Boston, 1923). The minister was Judge Hanna, then pastor of
the Boston Church. Cf. *Science and Health,* p. 79: "Jesus cast out
evil spirits, or false beliefs."

One might reply, man. But man, it will be recalled, has no body — since the body is material and matter does not exist. How about the souls of men? The word *souls*, we are told, must never be used in the plural:

> The term *souls* or *spirits* is as improper as the term *gods*. Soul or Spirit signifies Deity and nothing else. There is no finite soul nor spirit. Soul or Spirit means only one Mind, and cannot be rendered in the plural (p. 466).

If, however, there is no finite soul, and if Soul simply signifies Deity, it follows that man's soul was never created, but always existed. For God always existed, and man's Soul is equivalent to Deity. This point is, in fact, specifically stated: ". . . The universe, inclusive of man, is as eternal as God, who is its divine immortal Principle" (p. 554).

What, then, is creation for Christian Science? A perusal of Mrs. Eddy's commentary on Genesis (*Science and Health,* pp. 501-557) will reveal that she understands the creation narrative found in the first chapter of Genesis as referring simply to the unfolding of thoughts in the mind of God. Her comment on Genesis 1:1 has already been referred to: "This creation consists of the unfolding of spiritual ideas and their identities, which are embraced in the infinite Mind and forever reflected" (p. 503). We have also noted previously that the firmament of verse 6 is interpreted by her as meaning "spiritual understanding," and that the gathering together of the waters in verse 9 designates, for her, the gathering of unformed thoughts.[64] The dry land mentioned in verse 10 "illustrates the absolute formations instituted by Mind," whereas the water mentioned in this same verse "symbolizes the elements of Mind" (p. 507). When the 14th verse reports, "And God said, Let there be lights in the firmament of the heaven," Mrs. Eddy interprets as follows: "This text gives the idea of the rarefaction of thought as it ascends higher" (p. 509). When the creation of the two great lights is narrated in verse 16, however, the interpretation undergoes a slight shift: "The sun is a metaphorical representation of Soul outside the body, giving existence and intelligence to the universe" (p. 510).[65] On p. 511 we are told that rocks and mountains stand for solid and grand

---

[64] Pp. 505 and 506. See above, p. 25.
[65] Here Mrs. Eddy has slipped into a "mortal mind" way of thinking. If there is no such thing as body, as she contends, how can Soul be "outside the body"?

ideas, that animals and mortals represent the gradation of
mortal thought,[66] and that fowls that fly above the earth corres-
pond to aspirations soaring beyond and above corporeality (pp.
511-12). In connection with verse 26, where the creation of
man in God's image is recorded, Mrs. Eddy writes: "Man is
the family name for all ideas, — the sons and daughters of God"
(p. 515). And with respect to the command to be fruitful and
multiply (v. 28), the "scientific" interpretation is: "Divine Love
blesses its own ideas, and causes them to multiply. . ." (p. 517).

We conclude, therefore, that there is in Christian Science
teaching nothing even remotely resembling the Christian doctrine of creation. For Christian Scientists all that truly exists is
God. What we ordinarily think of as the material universe is simply
the thoughts of God. These thoughts, however, always existed.
Thus, for Christian Science, the narrative of creation in Genesis 1
is not a record of God's calling a universe into existence at a certain point of time, but simply an allegorical description of something which had no beginning (see p. 502) and will have no end
(see p. 503): the unfolding of the thoughts of God.

Providence. If we go by the sound of the words, it certainly
seems as if Christian Scientists believe in the providence of God —
that is, in God's continual preservation and government of the
universe. "God creates and governs the universe, including man,"
we read on page 295 of *Science and Health.* When we look up
the word *providence* in the concordances to Mrs. Eddy's writings,[67]
we find a number of places where the word is used. So, for
example, in her autobiography, called *Retrospection and Introspection,* we hear her saying, "Even so was I led into the mazes
of divine metaphysics through the gospel of suffering, the providence of God, and the cross of Christ."[68] In her Message to
the Mother Church at Boston for 1902, she began by saying,
"Beloved brethren, another year of God's loving providence for
His people in times of persecution has marked the history of

[66] But "mortal mind" is defined on p. 571 as "nothing claiming to be
something." Are animals and mortals, then, gradations of nothing?
Besides, Gen. 1 is supposed to be a "brief, glorious history of spiritual
creation," whereas the account which begins with 2:6 is said to be
"mortal and material" (p. 521). Why, then, this reference to *mortal
thought* in Genesis 1?

[67] Two of these concordances have been issued by the Christian Science
Church, one to *Science and Health,* and one to works other than *Science
and Health.* See bibliography.

[68] P. 30.

Christian Science."[69]   In another of her messages she urged her
people to "trust the divine Providence."[70]   In *Science and Health,*
in fact, she insists that "under divine Providence there can be
no accidents" (p. 424).

One of the aspects of divine providence is government.   We
note in Mrs. Eddy's writings many references to God's government. It is said, for instance, that "to fear sin is to misunderstand
the power of Love . . . to doubt His government and distrust
His omnipotent care" (p. 231).   On another page the following
advice is given: "Be firm in your understanding that the divine
Mind governs, and that in Science man reflects God's government"
(p. 393).   We find also frequent reference to God's government of
the universe.   "The term Science," we are told, "properly understood, refers only to the laws of God and to His government
of the universe, inclusive of man" (p. 128).   "The universe," it
is said, . . . is allied to divine Science as displayed in the ever-
lasting government of the universe" (p. 121).   On page 539 the
question is indignantly asked, "Has Spirit resigned to matter
the government of the universe?"

The other aspect of divine providence usually distinguished is
preservation.   We find occasional instances in which Mrs. Eddy
expresses belief in divine preservation.   For example, in *Christian
Science versus Pantheism* she says, "God, Spirit, is indeed the
preserver of man."[71]

When read at face value, these statements certainly give one
the impression that Christian Scientists accept the doctrine of
providence as taught by the historic Christian church.   However,
whenever we see the word God used in Christian Science literature, we must remember the definition of God cited earlier: "God
is All-in-all," and the implication of this definition: "nothing
possesses reality nor existence except the divine Mind and His
ideas" (above, p. 29).   If this is so, it is impossible for God
to govern or to preserve all, for God Himself is the all that is to
be governed or preserved.   If, now, we take another look at the
statement quoted from page 295 of *Science and Health,* "God
creates and governs the universe, including man," we recall
that there is, strictly speaking, no doctrine of creation in Christian

---

[69] *Message for 1902* (Boston, 1930), p. 1.
[70] *Miscellaneous Writings,* p. 320.
[71] P. 4 (Boston, 1926).

36   *Christian Science*

Science. So the first word used to describe God's activity here, *creates,* does not mean *creates* in the sense that Christians ordinarily understand creation, but means something completely different. The second word used to describe God's action here, however, the word *governs,* also does not at all mean what historic Christianity has always understood by that word. There can be no divine government in Christian Science (in the sense in which this word has usually been understood) since government implies that that which is governed is distinct from that which governs it. But this is precisely what is not the case in Christian Science. If God is all, how can he govern or preserve that which is identical with himself? If God is not a person but a principle, how can he (or it) be said to possess the kind of personal will necessary in one who governs or preserves? We conclude that there is, strictly speaking, no doctrine of divine providence in Christian Science, just as there is no doctrine of creation.

The above discussion illustrates and confirms a point made by Walter R. Martin in one of his books:[72] one of the most important keys for the understanding of cultism is to keep in mind the fact that cultists use the terminology of orthodox Christianity but pour into it a completely different meaning. We have noted how Christian Scientists do this in their usage of such terms as God, the Trinity, creation, and providence. We shall see more examples of this deceptive technique as we go along. The important lesson to be learned from this is that we may never assume, when a cultist uses a theological expression which sounds familiar, that he means by it what historic Christianity has always meant by it. One must always go beneath the word used to the concept for which it stands, if one would understand what the cultist is saying.

DOCTRINE OF MAN

According to Christian Science teaching, man has not fallen into sin; hence we cannot employ the customary distinction between man in his original state, and man in the state of sin. Accordingly, our subdivisions here will differ from those previously used.

---

[72] *The Christian and the Cults* (Grand Rapids: Zondervan, 1956), pp. 44-54.

THE CONSTITUTIONAL NATURE OF MAN

Man Has No Body. As we have seen, for Christian Scientists matter does not exist. This means that man has no body; the common belief that we have bodies is simply an error of mortal mind. "Spirit is God, and man is His image and likeness. Therefore man is not material; he is spiritual."[73] A more complete statement of this point is found in *Science and Health*:

> Man is not matter; he is not made up of brain, blood, bones, and other material elements. The Scriptures inform us that man is made in the image and likeness of God. Matter is not that likeness. . . . Man is spiritual and perfect. . . . He is . . . the reflection of God, or Mind, and therefore is eternal; that which has no separate mind from God; that which has not a single quality underived from Deity; that which possesses no life, intelligence, nor creative power of his own, but reflects spiritually all that belongs to his Maker (p. 475).

According to the above, man is not material in any sense; he has no bones, no blood, no material elements whatsoever. One may counter at this point: But does not the Bible say that man was formed from the dust of the ground? Christian Scientists reply that the verse which so describes man's formation (Gen. 2:7) is taken from the inferior Jehovistic document, so that this account of creation is therefore false and in error (see above, p. 24). No Christian Scientist, therefore, believes that man was made from the dust: "The belief that life can be in matter or soul in body, and that man springs from dust or from an egg, is the result of the mortal error which Christ, or Truth, destroys . . ." (p. 485).

The Image of God. Genesis 1, however, which according to Mrs. Eddy is the true, spiritual account of creation, pictures man as having been made in the image of God. What, now, do Christian Scientists understand by the image of God? That man is the image and reflection of God, particularly in the fact that he is spirit, not matter.

> Jesus taught but one God, one Spirit, who makes man in the image and likeness of Himself, — of Spirit, not of matter. Man reflects infinite Truth, Life, and Love. The nature of man, thus understood, includes all that is implied by the terms "image" and "likeness" as used in Scripture (p. 94).

> If the material body is man, he is a portion of matter, or dust. On the contrary, man is the image and likeness of Spirit; and

the belief that there is Soul in sense or Life in matter obtains in mortals, *alias* mortal mind, to which the apostle refers when he says that we must "put off the old man" (p. 172). The Scriptures inform us that man is made in the image and likeness of God. Matter is not that likeness. The likeness of Spirit cannot be so unlike Spirit (p. 475).

Summarizing, the constitutional nature of man, according to Christian Science, is that man is only spirit or soul, and that he has no material body. "The great mistake of mortals," says Mrs. Eddy, "is to suppose that man, God's image and likeness, is both matter and spirit, both good and evil" (p. 216). On another page, after affirming that Christian Science brings to light the only true God, and man as made in His likeness, she adds, "the opposite belief — that man originates in matter and has beginning and end, that he is both soul and body, both good and evil, both spiritual and material — terminates in discord and mortality, in the error which must be destroyed by Truth" (p. 338).[74]

THE SINLESSNESS OF MAN

The Fall of Man Denied. Christian Scientists deny that man has ever fallen into sin. "If man was once perfect but has now lost his perfection, then mortals have never beheld in man the reflex image of God" (p. 259). "In Science there is no fallen state of being; for therein is no inverted image of God. . . ."[75] What, then, do Christian Scientists do with the Biblical story of the fall recorded in Genesis 3? To begin with, they ascribe the fall narrative to a portion of Genesis which is said to be a myth (p. 530), and a history of error (p. 530). Further, they completely allegorize the account of the fall. Adam, for them, does not designate a historical person, but is a synonym for error, and stands for a belief of material mind (p. 529). Eve stands for "a finite belief concerning life, substance, and intelligence in

---

[74] It is interesting to note that Mormons and Christian Scientists arrive at opposite conclusions about the meaning of the image of God. Mormons contend that the term "image of God" applies primarily to man's physical nature, taking issue with those who see in it a reference to man's spiritual nature (see *The Four Major Cults*, pp. 48-49). Christian Scientists, on the other hand, see in the expression a repudiation of man's physical, bodily existence. Both interpretations are erroneous. For a thorough and competent recent study of the concept, the reader is referred to G. C. Berkouwer's *Man, the Image of God* (Eerdmans, 1962).
[75] *No and Yes* (Boston, 1936), p. 17.

matter" (p. 585). The serpent is at one time identified with corporeal sense (p. 533), and at another time interpreted as standing for "a lie . . . the first claim that sin, sickness, and death are the realities of life" (p. 594). The tree of life is explained as being "significant of eternal reality or being" (p. 538); whereas the tree of knowledge is said to typify unreality (p. 538). The fall, therefore, for Christian Science, was not a historical event; the Biblical narrative of it is simply an allegory picturing what is unreal and untrue in contrast to what is real and true — namely, the sinlessness of man. Their position is well summarized in the following words: "Whatever indicates the fall of man . . . is the Adam-dream, which is neither Mind nor man, for it is not begotten of the Father" (p. 282).

Man's Sinfulness Denied. Not only do Christian Scientists deny what theologians call original sin, however; they deny the existence of all sin, actual as well as original. For them there is no such thing as sin or evil. "Here also is found . . . the cardinal point in Christian Science, that matter and evil (including all inharmony, sin, disease, death) are *unreal.*"[76] ". . . Evil is naught, and good only is reality."[77] "Man is incapable of sin, sickness, and death. The real man cannot depart from holiness. . ." (p. 475).

When, therefore, we think we sin, or see someone else sin, we are simply the victims of an illusion: the illusion of mortal mind. Where mortal mind, which reveals its presence universally, comes from, however, Christian Scientists do not tell us. It cannot come from the fall of man, for there never was a fall. The persistence of mortal mind and of mortal thinking is one of the greatest mysteries in Christian Science. If all is God and God is all, mortal mind simply should not be — and yet it is!

Man Identified with God. We have already noted that, according to Mrs. Eddy, man "has no separate mind from God" (p. 475). This means that man is actually a part of God — which is already implied in their basic premise, "Whatever is, is God." We may say that, insofar as man is real, he is God; insofar as he is not God, he does not really exist. "The Science of being reveals man as perfect, even as the Father is perfect, because the Soul, or Mind, of the spiritual man is God, the divine Principle of all being. . ." (p. 302). "According to divine Science, man is in a

76 *Miscellaneous Writings,* p. 27.
77 *Unity of Good,* p. 21.

degree as perfect as the Mind that forms him" (p. 337). So
far is this identity carried that it is even said that whatever
God can do, man can do: "Man is God's image and likeness;
whatever is possible to God, is possible to man *as God's reflection.*"[78]

One wonders on what legitimate basis a Christian Scientist could
distinguish between man as he understands him and God. Since
God and man are equal, why should God be exalted above man?
Christian Science, by equating man and God, completely wipes
away the distinction between the creature and the Creator.

THE TIMELESSNESS OF MAN

It has become customary in Christian theology to distinguish
between God as the timeless one and man as a creature subject
to the limitations of time. This distinction, however, does not
hold in Christian Science. Man himself is a timeless being. In
connection with the doctrine of creation we noted that man had
no beginning in time; his soul is identical with Soul with a
capital letter, which signifies deity — hence man is as eternal as
God. This point is specifically stated on page 79 of *Miscellaneous
Writings*: "The spiritual man is that perfect and unfallen likeness,
coexistent and coeternal with God." Note also these words from
Science and Health: ". . . Let us remember that harmonious and
immortal man has existed forever, and is always beyond and
above the mortal illusion of any life, substance, and intelligence as
existent in matter" (p. 302).

This means that man's birth was not a real occurrence, but
only an illusion. "The belief that life can be in matter or soul
in body, and that man springs from . . . an egg, is the result of . . .
mortal error" (p. 485). "Can there be any birth or death for
man, the spiritual image and likeness of God?" (p. 206). "It
[Christian Science] brings to light the only living and true God
and man as made in His likeness; whereas the opposite belief —
that man originates in matter and has beginning and end . . . —
terminates in discord and mortality, in the error which must be
destroyed by Truth" (p. 338).[79]

[78] *Miscellaneous Writings,* p. 183.
[79] In view of the illusory nature of man's birth, it seems strange that
Mrs. Eddy found it necessary to give her students instructions as to the
proper way to attend the birth of a new child (p. 463).

So, for Christian Science, the real man is not the person who was born at such and such a time and who dies on such and such a day, but someone who is utterly timeless: who has always existed and will always exist. Since death is not real, as we have seen, there is no point at which man ceases to exist. Man had no beginning and will have no end. This man is not a being who can be perceived by ordinary eyes; his existence can only be discerned by faith: Christian Science faith, that is. We conclude that Christian Science, in its anthropology, denies the reality of the body, of sin and the fall, and repudiates man's temporality and finiteness.

DOCTRINE OF CHRIST

THE PERSON OF CHRIST

The Distinction between Jesus and Christ. As is well known, Jesus is the personal name of Christ (Mt. 1:21), whereas Christ is his official name, the name which designates His office (Mt. 16:16). The name Christ is the Greek equivalent of the Hebrew word *mashiach,* meaning *the Anointed One.* These two names frequently occur together in the New Testament, sometimes as Jesus Christ, sometimes as Christ Jesus.

In the first two centuries of the Christian era there were individuals and groups who distinguished sharply between Jesus, thought of as a mere man, and Christ, thought of as a divine spirit who descended upon Jesus at the time of his baptism and then left him again before He died.[80] Christian Scientists, though not at all agreeing with these groups in the way the distinction is made, nevertheless do share with them a sharp distinction between what they call Jesus and what they call Christ. Jesus, for them, was a certain man who lived in Palestine about 1900 years ago, whereas Christ is the name for a certain divine idea.[81]

[80] For example, the Ebionites, Cerinthus, and certain of the Gnostics. See Reinhold Seeberg, *Textbook of the History of Doctrines,* trans. Chas. Hay (Grand Rapids: Baker, 1954), I, 88, 92, 96-97.
[81] Already at this point we have our problems with this distinction. For, as we have just learned, the real man has no beginning and no end; neither birth nor death are real. How, then, can Christian Scientists speak of a certain man who lived in Palestine many years ago? Such a statement implies that, in the case of Christ at least, birth and death were real. Further, we have also learned that nothing really exists except the divine Mind and His ideas (above, p. 29). If this is so, the man Jesus could only truly exist as either part of the Divine Mind or as one of God's ideas. But if this is so, what is the difference between the

Let us look at some of the evidence for this distinction. "The spiritual Christ was infallible; Jesus, as material manhood, was not Christ."[82] "In healing the sick and sinning, Jesus elaborated the fact that the healing effect followed the understanding of the divine Principle and of the Christ-spirit which governed the corporeal Jesus" (p. 141). A more elaborate statement of the distinction is found on p. 473:

> Christ is the ideal Truth, that comes to heal sickness and sin through Christian Science, and attributes all power to God. Jesus is the name of the man who, more than all other men, has presented Christ, the true idea of God. . . . Jesus is the human man, and Christ is the divine idea; hence the duality of Jesus the Christ.

Looking at this distinction a bit more closely, we go on to ask ourselves, Who, then, is Christ — or, more accurately, what, then, is Christ — for Christian Science? He is "the spiritual or true idea of God" (p. 347); "Christ, as the true spiritual idea, is the ideal of God now and forever. . ." (p. 361). So — and this is very important for the understanding of Christian Science Christology — Christ is not a person, but merely an idea.

Who, then, is Jesus? A "human man," as we saw above. Jesus was a man who lived at a certain time. "Remember Jesus, who nearly nineteen centuries ago demonstrated the power of Spirit. . ." (p. 93). "This healing power of Truth must have been far anterior to the period in which Jesus lived" (p. 146). "The corporeal man Jesus was human" (p. 332).[83]

What, now, is the relation between these two: Jesus and Christ? One way of putting this would be to say that the invisible Christ became perceptible in the visible Jesus:

> The invisible Christ was imperceptible to the so-called personal senses, whereas Jesus appeared as a bodily existence. This dual

---

real Jesus and Christ (who is supposed to be a divine idea)? If Christian Scientists were consistent, they should repudiate the very distinction just alluded to. We shall find them maintaining this distinction with great difficulty.

[82] *Miscellaneous Writings*, p. 84.

[83] So far the distinction seems to be somewhat clear: Jesus was a man whereas Christ was an idea or concept. In the Glossary of *Science and Health*, however, we find Mrs. Eddy wreaking havoc with her own distinction, when she tells us that Jesus means "the highest human corporeal concept of the divine idea. . ." (p. 589). Previously Jesus had been defined as a man; now he is only a concept! We see, thus, that the distinction between Jesus and Christ is already breaking down.

personality of the unseen and the seen, the spiritual and material, the eternal Christ and the corporeal Jesus manifest in the
flesh, continued until the Master's ascension. . . (p. 334).[84]

This does not mean, however, that the invisible Christ was not
in the world previous to Jesus' appearance "as a bodily existence."
"Throughout all generations both before and after the Christian
era, the Christ, as the spiritual idea . . . has come with some
measure of power and grace to all prepared to receive Christ,
Truth" (p. 333). If Christ was in the world before the Christian
era, what, then, did the man Jesus do? "Jesus demonstrated
Christ; he proved that Christ is the divine idea of God — the
Holy Ghost, or Comforter, revealing the divine Principle, Love,
and leading into all truth" (p. 332).[85] At the time of the
ascension, we are told, "the human, material concept, or Jesus,
disappeared, while the spiritual self, or Christ,[86] continues to
exist in the eternal order of divine Science, taking away the sins
of the world, as the Christ has always done, even before the
human Jesus was incarnate to mortal eyes" (p. 334).

Summing up the relation between Jesus and Christ, Jesus
was a man (or a concept) who presented and demonstrated
Christ, a divine idea (or a spiritual self). Sometimes it is Jesus
who is the person and Christ which is the impersonal idea, and
then again it is Jesus which is the impersonal concept and Christ
who is the spiritual self. If the going seems a bit rough here,
the reader is reminded that this is but a small sample of the difficulty one encounters when he tries to determine exactly what Christian Scientists teach.

Is Jesus still alive? He should be, since, according to Christian
Science teaching, there is no death and man has no beginning
or end. Yet, in the passage just cited from page 334, Mrs. Eddy
says that, at the time of the ascension, "the human, material concept, or Jesus, disappeared." In the light of this statement we
must assume that Jesus has simply been annihilated. Mrs. Eddy
also denies that the human Jesus was or is eternal (p. 333-34).
The only conclusion we can arrive at is that the human Jesus
no longer exists. As a matter of fact, we may as well say that,

---

[84] How could the corporeal Jesus be manifest in the flesh if, as Mrs.
Eddy teaches, nothing corporeal really exists?

[85] Here we are told that Christ is the Holy Ghost. Thus further
confusion is introduced into Christian Science teaching about the Trinity.

[86] Note that, according to this quotation, Jesus is a concept and Christ
is a self, thus completely reversing the definitions previously given!

for Christian Science, there never was a Jesus.   For Jesus was
supposed to have been "a corporeal man"; for Christian science,
however, corporeality does not really exist.

A Jesus who has been reduced to such small dimensions could
not have been a very important person.   That this was so for
Mrs. Eddy is conclusively proved by the following statement which
she once made in one of her classes:

> If there had never existed such a person as the Galilean Prophet,
> it would make no difference to me.   I should still know that
> God's spiritual ideal is the only real man in His image and like-
> ness.[87]

The Jesus of Christian Science, therefore, was so insignificant that
if he had not lived, it would have made no essential difference!
What was important about Jesus was the idea he had.   Though
Jesus is no more, the idea he presented and demonstrated is
still in the world, in the teachings of Christian Science.   Christian
Science is therefore actually more important than the man Jesus!

The Incarnation and the Virgin Birth.   Was there a real
incarnation?   Did the Word truly become flesh?   Since, according
to Christian Scientists, there is no such thing as matter, how
can they conceive of God's having entered into a material body?
We are not surprised to find them flatly denying the possibility of
the incarnation: "A portion of God could not enter man; neither
could God's fulness be reflected by a single man, else God would
be manifestly finite, lose the deific character, and become less than
God" (p. 336).

Was Jesus born of a virgin?   Yes, says Christian Science, but
not in a crassly material way:

> Those instructed in Christian Science have reached the glorious
> perception that God is the only author of man.   The Virgin-
> mother conceived this idea of God, and gave to her ideal the
> name of Jesus. . . .
>
> The illumination of Mary's spiritual sense put to silence ma-
> terial law and its order of generation, and brought forth her
> child by the revelation of Truth, demonstrating God as the
> Father of man (p. 29).
>
> Jesus was the offspring of Mary's self-conscious communion
> with God (pp. 29-30).
>
> Mary's conception of him [Jesus] was spiritual . . . (p. 332).

It is admittedly difficult to follow Mrs. Eddy's reasoning here.

[87] *The First Church of Christ, Scientist, and Miscellany,* pp. 318-19.

If we read the first two sentences carefully, we get the impression that what Mary conceived was an idea, rather than a flesh-and-blood son. This position is, however, not consistent with expressions which speak of Jesus as a human man (p. 473) and as manifest in the flesh (p. 334). Neither is this position consistent with the distinction between Jesus and Christ. For Christ was supposed to be the divine idea, and Jesus a corporeal man, whereas it now turns out that Jesus was just an idea after all.

The Fallibility of Jesus. Although the Bible teaches the complete sinlessness of our Lord Jesus Christ, Mrs. Eddy contends that Jesus was fallible, deceptive, and in error on certain points. It will be recalled that, according to her, it was only the spiritual Christ who was infallible, since Jesus, as material manhood, was not Christ.[88] Note further the following statements:

> He [Jesus] knew the mortal errors which constitute the material body, and could destroy those errors; but at the time when Jesus felt our infirmities, he had not conquered all the beliefs of the flesh or his sense of material life, nor had he risen to his final demonstration of spiritual power (p. 53).
>
> Sometimes Jesus called a disease by name. . . . These instances show the concessions which Jesus was willing to make to the popular ignorance of spiritual Life-laws (p. 398).
>
> To accommodate himself to immature ideas of spiritual power, — for spirituality was possessed only in a limited degree even by his disciples, — Jesus called the body, which by spiritual power he raised from the grave, "flesh and bones" (p. 313).

Summing up, according to the quotation from page 53, Jesus, while on earth, entertained some "beliefs of the flesh" — which, so Christian Science teaches, are erroneous beliefs; according to the statement from page 398, Jesus deepened "the popular ignorance" instead of removing it; and, according to the assertion found on page 313, Jesus actually told an untruth in order to accommodate himself to his disciples' immature ideas. The Jesus of Christian Science, therefore, was either not sufficiently mature to have overcome erroneous beliefs, or not sufficiently frank to acknowledge his rejection of such beliefs. In other words, he was either the victim of error, or deliberately dishonest and deceptive. Is this the Christ of the Scriptures?

It is highly significant that whenever Jesus and Mrs. Eddy

---

[88] *Miscellaneous Writings,* p. 84.

disagree (as, for example, on the matter of the reality of disease), it is Jesus who is wrong and Mrs. Eddy who is right.

The Deity of Jesus. After what has been said, it need hardly be added that Christian Science denies the full deity of Jesus. It will be recalled that he is called a human man, a corporeal man, and so on. The admission of the fallibility of Jesus certainly denies his equality with God. Mrs. Eddy particularly takes up the question of Jesus' deity on page 361 of *Science and Health*:

> The Christian who believes in the First Commandment is a monotheist. Thus he virtually unites with the Jew's belief in one God, and recognizes that Jesus Christ is not God, as Jesus himself declared, but is the Son of God. This declaration of Jesus, understood, conflicts not at all with another of his sayings: "I and my Father are one," — that is, one in quality, not in quantity. As a drop of water is one with the ocean, a ray of light one with the sun, even so God and man, Father and son, are one in being.

Two things are evident from this quotation. First, Jesus is not considered fully equal to God; the term *Son of God* here is intended to mean something less than full equality with God. Second, insofar as Jesus is here said to be "one in being" with God the Father, he is so in no different way than any one of us is, since, as we have seen, what gives all of us reality is the fact that we are part of God (as the water is part of the ocean). We conclude, therefore, that Christian Science denies the unique deity of Jesus Christ.

Other Doctrines Denied. Nowhere do we see the completely anti-Christian character of Christian Science teaching as clearly as in its doctrine of Christ. Not just *some* but *all* the major elements of the Christology of historic Christianity are repudiated by this group. We have already noted a number of these; let us look at a few more examples.

According to Christian Science, *Jesus did not have a genuine human nature.* Though Mrs. Eddy says that the corporeal man Jesus was human (p. 332), and that Jesus appeared as a bodily existence (p. 334), on another page she explains what this "bodily existence" amounted to: "Wearing in part a human form (that is, as it seemed to mortal view), being conceived by a human mother, Jesus was the mediator between Spirit and the flesh, between Truth and error" (p. 315). Here the humanity

of Jesus is first said to have been only partial, and later asserted
to have been only a seeming one: "as it seemed to mortal view."
Since *mortal mind,* according to the Glossary, is "error creating
other errors" (p. 591), we may conclude that *mortal view* is
an erroneous view. The thought that Jesus had a human form
is, therefore, one of the errors of mortal mind which must be
laid aside if we desire to understand the truth.

Further, *Jesus did not really suffer.* Though we are told
on page 11 that "Jesus suffered for our sins," we are informed
on page 23 that "suffering is an error of sinful sense."

Again, *Jesus did not really die.* "Jesus' students," Mrs.
Eddy tells us, ". . . did not perform many wonderful works, until
they saw him after his crucifixion and learned that he had not
died" (pp. 45-46). Farther down on the same page she speaks
of "Jesus' unchanged physical condition after what seemed to
be death" (p. 46). Jesus' death, therefore, was not real but
only apparent. He was alive all the time he was in the tomb,
doing a very important three days' work, namely, solving the
great problem of being (p. 44). Nevertheless, with a sublime dis-
regard for all the laws of logic, Mrs. Eddy informs us, on page
45, that "our Master fully and finally demonstrated divine Science
in his victory over death and the grave." A stupendous victory
this was: over a death which had never occurred, and over a
grave which never held a dead body!

Jesus did not really arise from the dead. "Our Master," we
read on page 509, "reappeared to his students, — to their apprehension he arose from the grave, — on the third day of his
ascending thought. . . ." Note that he reappeared only to the
apprehension of his students, and that he did so, not on the
third day of his sojourn in the tomb, but on the third day of
his *ascending thought.* If his thought had been ascending for
three days, he was not really dead, and hence this was not really
a resurrection. On page 201 of *Miscellaneous Writings* we find
Mrs. Eddy saying, "When Jesus reproduced his body after its
burial, he revealed the myth or material falsity of evil. . . ."
Whereas the Bible teaches the physical resurrection of Jesus
Christ from the dead, Mrs. Eddy contends that Jesus merely
reproduced his body. Since Jesus' human form, or partial human
form, was only one that seemed to be such to erring, mortal view,
we may conclude that he had no real bodily existence before his
death. The "reproduction" after his burial, therefore, can only

mean that Jesus reproduced for his disciples the appearance of a body.[89] When we turn to the definition of *resurrection* found in the Glossary, we read, "Spiritualization of thought; a new and higher idea of immortality, or spiritual existence; material belief yielding to spiritual understanding" (p. 593). Spiritualization of thought, however, is not the resurrection of a dead body; thus this pivotal doctrine of Biblical Christianity is also flatly denied.

Jesus did not really ascend into heaven. "This dual personality of . . . the eternal Christ and the corporeal Jesus manifest in flesh, continued until the Master's ascension, when the human, material concept, or Jesus, disappeared. . ." (p. 334). According to this statement, what ascended was not a person but merely an idea: the human concept disappeared. Another explanation of the ascension tells us: "In his final demonstration, called the ascension, which closed the earthly record of Jesus, he arose above the physical knowledge of his disciples, and the material senses saw him no more" (p. 46). So here the ascension is interpreted as meaning that the material senses of his disciples no longer saw him;[90] this was not an ascension into heaven, therefore, but simply a rising above his disciples' physical knowledge. Still another interpretation of the ascension is found on the same page: ". . . After his resurrection he [Jesus] proved to the physical senses that his body was not changed until he himself ascended, — or, in other words, rose even higher in the understanding of Spirit, God." The expression, *in other words,* tells us that what follows is an explanation of what the ascension meant: Christ's rising higher in the understanding of Spirit. In none of these three conflicting interpretations of the ascension, however, do we find the faintest resemblance to the Biblical teaching that Christ actually went up to heaven in His glorified body; thus this doctrine, too, is discarded by Christian Scientists.[91]

In summary, Christian Science denies the unity of the Person

[89] But why should he have done this, if one purpose of his ministry, as Mrs. Eddy maintains, was to reveal the unreality of matter?

[90] This is also a perplexing statement. According to p. 313 Jesus called the body he had raised from the grave "flesh and bones" only to accommodate himself to the immaturity of his disciples. In other words, this was not a material body. But now his ascension is said to mean that the material senses of his disciples no longer saw him whose body was not really material in the first place!

[91] For Christian Science teaching on the Second Coming of Christ, see the section dealing with their doctrine of the last things.

of Jesus Christ, Jesus' present existence, the absolute necessity for Jesus' earthly mission, the incarnation of Christ, the Virgin birth of Jesus, the sinlessness of Jesus, the full deity of Jesus, and Jesus' genuine humanity. In addition, it rejects Jesus' suffering, death, physical resurrection, and ascension into heaven. By what conceivable right, therefore, do the members of this group still dare to call themselves a church of *Christ?*

THE WORK OF CHRIST

Jesus did not atone for our sin by shedding his blood on the cross. As we have seen, Christian Scientists reject Jesus' genuine humanity, his suffering, death, and resurrection. One cannot, therefore, expect to find them teaching that Jesus atoned for our sin, particularly not since they deny the reality of sin. The thought that Jesus Christ shed his blood on the cross in order to pay the debt incurred by our sin must have been particularly abhorrent to Mrs. Eddy, for we find her specifically disavowing it several times:

> The real atonement — so infinitely beyond the heathen conception that God requires human blood to propitiate His justice and bring His mercy — needs to be understood.[92]
> That God's wrath should be vented upon His beloved Son, is divinely unnatural (p. 23).
> One sacrifice, however great, is insufficient to pay the debt of sin (p. 23).
> The material blood of Jesus[93] was no more efficacious to cleanse from sin when it was shed upon "the accursed tree," than when it was flowing in his veins as he went daily about his Father's business (p. 25).

The work of Jesus was rather to demonstrate the truth. We have previously noted that, according to Christian Science teaching, Jesus came to present or to demonstrate a divine idea (*Science and Health,* pp. 473 and 332). In harmony with this, the significance of the crucifixion of Jesus is said to be that it demonstrated affection and goodness: "The efficacy of the crucifixion lay in the practical affection and goodness it demonstrated for mankind" (p. 24).[94]

---

92 *No and Yes,* p. 34.
93 A peculiar statement, to say the least, by a person who denies that anything material can exist.
94 We see here the attempt to treat the crucifixion as if it were something very real when actually, according to Christian Science teaching, it can-

Similar statements are made about the sufferings of Jesus: "It was not to appease the wrath of God, but to show the allness of Love and the nothingness of hate, sin, and death, that Jesus suffered."[95] "Was it just for Jesus to suffer? No; but it was inevitable, for not otherwise could he show us the way and the power of Truth" (p. 40).

More specifically, *the work of Jesus was to set us an example of the kind of life we must live.* "Jesus aided in reconciling man to God by giving man a truer sense of Love . . . and this truer sense of Love redeems man from the law of matter, sin, and death by the law of Spirit. . ." (p. 19). "His consummate example was for the salvation of us all, but only through doing the works which he did and taught others to do" (p. 51). "Jesus did his work, and left his glorious career for our example."[96] "Jesus taught the way of Life by demonstration . . ." (p. 25). "He did life's work aright not only in justice to himself, but in mercy to mortals, — to show them how to do theirs, but not to do it for them nor to relieve them of a single responsibility" (p. 18).

Typical of the Christian Science view of Jesus is the description of him as a "Way-shower": "This [his advent in the flesh] accounts for his [Jesus'] struggles in Gethsemane and on Calvary, and this enabled him to be the mediator, or *way-shower,* between God and men" (p. 30). "The Christ-element in the Messiah made him the Way-shower, Truth and Life" (p. 228).

What Christian Scientists therefore stress about Jesus is not his Person, but the impersonal example he set before us and the impersonal truth he represented: "Our heavenly Father, divine Love, demands that all men should follow the example of our Master and his apostles and not merely worship his personality" (p. 40).[97] "Christ is Truth, and Truth is always here, — the impersonal Saviour."[98] It is not the Person of Jesus who saves, but the principle for which he stands. Mrs. Eddy relegates those

---

not have been real. For if suffering and death are not real, how could there have been a real crucifixion? The only consistent interpretation of the above statement, on Christian Science premises, would be to say that affection and goodness were demonstrated by an illusion.

[95] *No and Yes,* p. 35. It will be recalled, however, that Mrs. Eddy said, on p. 23 of *Science and Health,* that suffering is "an error of sinful sense."

[96] *Miscellaneous Writings,* p. 212.

[97] Note that here the example of Jesus is not particularly distinguished from that of his apostles. In other words, there appears to be nothing unique about it.

[98] *Miscellaneous Writings,* p. 180.

who still cling to the Person of Jesus to the category of
scholasticism: "Scholasticism clings for salvation to the person,
instead of to the divine Principle, of the man Jesus. . ." (p. 146).

One could call the Christian Science view of the work of Jesus
the *Example* or *Moral Influence* theory of the atonement. Because
of the pecularities of Christian Science theology, however, their
view of the atonement does not really fit into any previous category.
The great difficulty in speaking of the Christian Science view of
the atonement is that, for them, sin has no real existence. If this
is so, how can one speak of an *atonement* in Christian Science?
How can one atone for something which does not exist?

It is clear that Christian Scientists repudiate the teaching which
is at the heart of the gospel: that Jesus Christ suffered and died
on the cross in order to bear the burden of God's wrath against
sin, so that we might be saved through His blood. We are left
with a Jesus who was merely an example — an example so impersonal, in fact, that it is the principle for which He stands
that saves rather than He Himself. In Christian Science one can
get along very well without the Person of Jesus Christ!

DOCTRINE OF SALVATION

Here again we face a real difficulty. How can you speak of
a doctrine of salvation in a system which denies that man is in
need of salvation? According to Christian Science, man is not a
sinner. If sin is not real, and if man has never fallen, what does
man need to be saved from? The most common answer Christian
Scientists give to this question is: from false beliefs. Yet this is
not the whole story, as we shall see. In their teachings on the
doctrine of salvation, as in so many other areas, we shall find
Christian Scientists hopelessly inconsistent.

We have previously noted that, according to Christian Science,
sin and evil have no real existence, but are only illusions (see
above, p. 27). In agreement with this view of sin, we read on
page 473 of *Science and Health* that Christ "came to destroy the
belief of sin." On another page Mrs. Eddy explains how we are
to rid ourselves of sin:

> To get rid of sin through Science, is to divest sin of any sup-
> posed mind or reality, and never to admit that sin can have
> intelligence or power, pain or pleasure. You conquer error by
> denying its verity (p. 339).

On the basis of statements of this sort, sin is just a bad dream, and we must all learn not to believe in bad dreams. Being "saved from sin," therefore, on these terms is simply ceasing to believe that sin has any reality.[99]

Here, too, however, we find Christian Scientists guilty of the grossest inconsistencies and contradictions. We have learned that sin, sickness, and death have no real existence but are illusions, and that man is incapable of sin, sickness, and death. Yet we are also told that the Master "wrought a full salvation from sin, sickness, and death" (p. 39), and that salvation means "sin, sickness, and death destroyed" (p. 593). If we take the last statement seriously, and understand *destroyed* to mean "have no real existence," we are shut up to two possibilities: either everyone possesses salvation (since, according to Christian Science, these three things have no real existence for anybody), or sin, sickness, and death are real after all and are destroyed only for certain people. If the first of these two alternatives is true, the word *salvation* has lost all meaning, being equivalent to mere existence. If the second is true, these three evils do exist in some sense, and Christian Science has lost its main plank.

It is extremely difficult to know exactly what Mrs. Eddy means; she keeps shifting from one position to another, until the reader begins to suffer from intellectual vertigo. If we, however, assume that the latter alternative is true — that sin, sickness, and death do have some kind of relative existence, and that salvation means to be delivered from them — how, then, is one saved from sin in Christian Science? The answer is very simple: one just quits sinning. "The way to escape the misery of sin is to cease sinning. There is no other way" (p. 327).[100] ". . . If the sinner continues

[99] The implications of this view of sin, when carried to their logical extreme, are appalling. On this basis, one could arise from the most wicked debauchery of which man's heart is capable, and simply brush off his guilt by saying, "There is no such thing as sin!" A more dangerous weapon than this teaching was never handed to depraved mankind!

[100] "To cease sinning" — what can this possibly mean? In view of previous statements about the unreality of sin, does this mean merely: stop thinking you are sinning? If so, one could blithely persist in theft and murder, or whatever else his depraved heart desired. If, however, at this point Mrs. Eddy means: stop doing wrong things, then sin has some reality after all, and the entire structure of Christian Science theology topples to the ground.

to pray and repent, sin[101] and be sorry, he has little part in the atonement, — in the *at-one-ment* with God, — for he lacks the practical repentance, which reforms the heart and enables man to do the will of wisdom" (p. 19).

When one further inquires, however, whether it is not possible in Christian Science to obtain forgiveness for sin, one receives the following answers:

> To remit the penalty due for sin, would be for Truth to pardon error. Escape from punishment is not in accordance with God's government, since justice is the handmaid of mercy (p. 36).
>
> Does not Science show that sin brings suffering as much today as yesterday? They who sin must suffer.[102] "With what measure ye mete, it shall be measured to you again" (p. 37).
>
> Justice requires reformation of the sinner. Mercy cancels the debt only when justice approves (p. 22).[103]

We are now so hopelessly trapped in the maze of Christian Science doubletalk that it does not seem as though we shall ever escape. Sin is supposed to be an illusion and a delusion; yet the only way one can avoid suffering and escape the penalty due to sin is to quit sinning! If one takes the last-quoted statements seriously, Christian Science appears to be unspeakably cruel and heartless. It seems to say: Quit your sinning completely, or else suffer the terrible penalties which your sin incurs.

No one need be very perturbed, however, by threatenings of this sort, because he can immediately turn to other pages in *Science and Health* to find statements which sound like this: "All that we term sin, sickness, and death is a mortal belief" (p.

---

[101] "If the sinner continues to sin. . . ." Meaning? How can he continue to do something of which he is incapable? Suppose I have just proved that man, not having wings like a bird, cannot fly. But now, after having proved this, I say, "If man, however, keeps on flying like a bird, he reveals his lack of true spirituality." Such a statement would make as much sense as Mrs. Eddy's affirmation about continuing in sin.

[102] Note how completely nonsensical this statement is, in the light of previous Christian Science teaching that both sin and suffering are unreal: "If one sins" (and to think that you can sin is an error of mortal sense), "one must suffer" (and to think that one can suffer is an error of sinful sense).

[103] It will be recalled that "sinner" is for Christian Scientists an impossible term to apply to man. How can one, now, *reform* a person who is incapable of sin? The term *debt*, in the latter part of the quotation, implies that some real sins have been committed. But there are no real sins, according to Christian Science teaching. How, then, can there be a debt which needs to be canceled?

278); "man is incapable of sin, sickness, and death" (p. 475); "sin, sickness, and death must be deemed as devoid of reality as they are of good . . ." (p. 525). So the sin which is said to bring suffering, to involve debt, and to make one liable to punishment, is just a false belief after all, and does not really exist.

We conclude, then, that for Christian Science salvation from sin is accomplished when one ceases to sin, or when one stops believing that there is such a thing as sin. In either event, the death of Christ has nothing to do with salvation; if Christ had never existed, it would have made no real difference. It is thus clear that Christian Science teaching on salvation bears not the slightest resemblance to the soteriology of historic Christianity, and has no right to call itself Christian.

DOCTRINE OF THE CHURCH AND SACRAMENTS

DOCTRINE OF THE CHURCH

In the Glossary of *Science and Health* the church is defined as follows:

> The structure of Truth and Love; whatever rests upon and proceeds from divine Principle.
> The Church is that institution, which affords proof of its utility and is found elevating the race, rousing the dormant understanding from material beliefs to the apprehension of spiritual ideas and the demonstration of divine Science, thereby casting out devils, or error, and healing the sick (p. 583).

From this definition it is obvious that, in common with all cults, Christian Science claims to be the only true church, thus implying that all other groups which call themselves churches are false. The position Christian Scientists take on Mrs. Eddy and her textbook already implicitly involves this claim. For, as we saw previously, they contend that Mrs. Eddy received the final revelation of the divine Principle of scientific mental healing (p. 107), and that *Science and Health* is the voice of truth, uncontaminated by human hypotheses (pp. 456-57). If this is so, it must follow that no group outside of Christian Science has or knows the truth.

This point is specifically stated by Mrs. Eddy: "Outside of Christian Science all is vague and hypothetical, the opposite of Truth. . ." (p. 545). Doctrines of churches other than the Christian Science Church are called man-made: Mrs. Eddy speaks of a time to come "when the lethargy of mortals, produced by man-made doctrines, is broken by the demands of divine Science" (p. 38). Note also these words:

> The notion of a material universe is utterly opposed to the theory of man as evolved from Mind. Such fundamental errors send falsity into all human doctrines and conclusions. . . (p. 545).

On the other hand, we are told, it is Christian Science which has brought truth to light: "Christian Science brings to light Truth and its supremacy, universal harmony, the entireness of God, good, and the nothingness of evil" (p. 293). The contrast between Christian Science and all mere "human beliefs" is highlighted in the following quotation:

> Beyond the frail premises of human beliefs, above the loosening grasp of creeds, the demonstration of Christian Mind-healing stands a revealed and practical Science. It is imperious throughout all ages as Christ's revelation of Truth, of Life, and of Love, which remains inviolate for every man to understand and to practice (p. 98).

We are further told that "Christian Science teaches only that which is spiritual and divine, and not human. Christian Science is unerring and Divine; the human sense of things errs because it is human" (p. 99). When Christian Science is, moreover, completely identified with Christianity (p. 372),[104] we are left with no alternative but that of concluding that any group which does not agree with Christian Science is, in its judgment, not genuinely Christian.

It is quite clear that there is in Christian Science, as in Mormonism, no appreciation for the doctrine of the universal church. The only true church, according to them, is the Christian Science Church; all others flounder about in error and in darkness.

DOCTRINE OF THE SACRAMENTS

It could be expected that Christian Scientists would find the sacraments, in which spiritual truths are expressed through material means, rather embarrassing. As a matter of fact, Christian Scientists have simply eliminated the sacraments from their services.

[104] "Christian Science and Christianity are one."

56   *Christian Science*

Baptism. There is no rite of baptism in Christian Science Churches, either for infants or for adults:

> Christian Science has one faith, one Lord, one baptism; and this faith builds on Spirit, not matter; and this baptism is the purification of mind, — not an ablution of the body, but tears of repentance, an overflowing love, washing away the motives for sin; yea, it is love leaving self for God.[105]

Baptism is therefore defined in the Glossary of *Science and Health* as follows: "Purification by Spirit; submergence in Spirit" (p. 581). Repeating this thought in slightly different words, Mrs. Eddy says elsewhere: "Our baptism is a purification from all error" (p. 35). In Chapter VII of *Miscellaneous Writings* Mrs. Eddy speaks of three senses in which Christian Scientists may be said to receive baptism: the baptism of repentance, the baptism of the Holy Ghost, and the baptism of Spirit;[106] nowhere, however, does she mention water-baptism.

The Lord's Supper. Christian Scientists do not administer the Lord's Supper at their services. They do hold so-called communion services in the branch churches twice a year,[107] but on these occasions neither bread nor wine is served.

Thomas L. Leishman explains the Christian Science position on this point as follows:

> To all Christian Scientists, *Communion* — in thought and in practice — possesses a deep and abiding significance, but, as in the case of baptism, we seek to attain to the *spiritual* meaning of the Eucharist, dispensing with the literal use of sacramental bread and wine, as we dispense with the use of actual baptismal water.[108]

The use of bread and wine, Mrs. Eddy teaches, hinders one from understanding the spiritual sense of the sacrament: "The true sense is spiritually lost, if the sacrament is confined to the use of bread and wine" (p. 32).[109]

[105] Mary Baker Eddy, *The People's Idea of God* (Boston, 1936), p. 9.
[106] Pp. 203-205. One wonders why the baptism of Spirit is different from that of the Holy Ghost.
[107] At first, communion services were also held in the Mother Church, but Mrs. Eddy abolished these services in 1908. The reason she gave was: the number of communicants had grown so great that the church could no longer seat them (Dakin, *op. cit.*, p. 505).
[108] *Why I Am a Christian Scientist* (New York: Nelson, 1958), p. 87.
[109] Note that Mrs. Eddy thus arbitrarily removes from the Lord's Supper the very element which makes it a sacrament: the outward and visible material sign.

Typical of Mrs. Eddy's spiritualizing exegesis is her reinterpretation of the Biblical record of Christ's last supper:

> His followers, sorrowful and silent, anticipating the hour of their Master's betrayal, partook of the heavenly manna, which of old had fed in the wilderness the persecuted followers of Truth. Their bread indeed came down from heaven. It was the great truth of spiritual being, healing the sick and casting out error. Their Master had explained it all before, and now this bread was feeding and sustaining them. They had borne this bread from house to house, *breaking* (explaining) it to others, and now it comforted themselves (p. 33).

For Mrs. Eddy, therefore, the bread of the last supper was the truth of spiritual being, and Jesus' breaking of the bread simply meant that he was explaining his truth to his disciples. The entire Lord's Supper, therefore, is to be understood not in a material but in a spiritual manner:

> Our Eucharist is spiritual communion with the one God. Our bread, "which cometh down from heaven," is Truth. Our cup is the cross. Our wine the inspiration of Love, the draught our Master drank and commended to his followers (p. 35).

What kind of "communion service" do Christian Scientists hold in their branch churches? As was said, no bread or wine is served. At a certain point in the service, however, the congregation is invited to kneel in silent communion.[110] Leishman explains that this period of silent communion is one "during which we seek to realize more fully our union and spiritual relationship with Him, with a view to becoming better Christians — and Christian Scientists."[111]

When this service of silent communion is held, however, Christian Scientists do not commemorate the Last Supper of our Lord, but rather the "morning meal" which Jesus shared with His disciples after His resurrection, on the shore of the Sea of Tiberias.

> What a contrast between our Lord's last supper and his last spiritual breakfast with his disciples in the bright morning hours at the joyful meeting on the shore of the Galilean Sea! . . . This spiritual meeting with our Lord in the dawn of a new light is the morning meal which Christian Scientists commemorate. . . . They celebrate their Lord's victory over death, his probation in the flesh after death, its exemplification of human probation,

110 *Church Manual*, p. 126.
111 *Op. cit.*, p. 91.

and his spiritual and final ascension above matter, or the flesh, when he rose out of material sight (p. 35).

We learn from Leishman that it is at the communion service that this "morning meal" is commemorated.[112]

It need hardly be added that a period of silent meditation such as described above, though it may be spiritually helpful, is no sacrament.   Christ Himself instituted the sacraments for the strengthening of our faith; Christian Scientists, however, do not find them necessary.   Once again we have found Mrs. Eddy claiming to be wiser than Jesus Christ Himself.

DOCTRINE OF THE LAST THINGS

In expounding Christian Science teachings about the last things, it is impossible to make the customary distinction between individual eschatology (the soul after death) and general eschatology (events associated with the Second Coming of Christ). For, as we shall see, there is no such thing as general eschatology in Christian Science.   It will be recalled that, according to Mrs. Eddy, "nothing possesses reality nor existence except the divine Mind and His ideas" (p. 331).   If the universe is thus nothing other than the divine Mind and His ideas, it follows that the universe can have no cataclysmic end or transformation, that history can have no climax, and that things must simply go on and on as they do now (or, rather, appear to go on and on, for in a pantheistic system like Christian Science there can be no real history).   Since Jesus, as we have seen, neither really arose from the dead nor really ascended into heaven, he cannot return to earth in a Second Coming.   It is obvious, therefore, that there can be no general eschatology in Christian Science teaching.

Christian Scientists do teach a kind of individual eschatology, though in this area, as in all others, their views are radically different from the teachings of historic Christianity.[113]   Actually, their chief emphasis is on salvation as a present experience rather than as a future possession:

[112] *Ibid.,* p. 92.

[113] Customarily, individual eschatology deals with the state of the soul between death and the resurrection. Christian Scientists, however, deny the reality of both death and the resurrection. It is therefore to be expected that their views on man's state after "the change called death" will be in a class by themselves.

"Now," cried the apostle, "is the accepted time; behold, *now* is the day of salvation," — meaning, not that now men must prepare for a future-world salvation, or safety, but that now is the time in which to experience that salvation in spirit and in life (p. 39).

Though this is so, Christian Scientists will grant that salvation cannot be limited to this present life, since there is an existence after this life:

> Man is not annihilated, nor does he lose his identity, by passing through the belief called death. After the momentary belief of dying passes from mortal mind, this mind is still in a conscious state of existence. . . .[114]

A Time of Probation. Mrs. Eddy teaches that after "the change called death" there will be a time of probation for everyone. "As death findeth mortal man, so shall he be after death, until probation and growth shall effect the needed change" (p. 291). We may not assume, therefore, that death automatically destroys the illusion that matter, sickness, and sin exist.

> If the change called *death* destroyed the belief in sin, sickness, and death, happiness would be won at the moment of dissolution, and be forever permanent; but this is not so. Perfection is gained only by perfection. . . .
>
> The sin and error which possess us at the instant of death do not cease at that moment, but endure until the death of these errors (p. 290).[115]

This means, then, that some kind of spiritual progress is necessary for every man after "the change called death." This progress is called "growth."

> The period required for this dream of material life, embracing its so-called pleasures and pains, to vanish from consciousness, "knoweth no man . . . neither the Son, but the Father." This

---

[114] *Miscellaneous Writings*, p. 42. Note that death is described as a mere belief, and that "mortal mind" does not die but continues to persist after the "change called death." Mortal mind is thus possessed of some kind of immortality.

[115] This quotation well illustrates the "Alice-in-Wonderland" quality of Christian Science double talk. One of the basic tenets of Christian Science is that neither death nor matter have any real existence; yet here Mrs. Eddy speaks of "the moment of dissolution." The bewildered reader is bound to ask, "Dissolution of what?" It cannot be the body, for there is no body. Neither can it be the soul, for the soul is part of God. Christian Science also teaches that sin is an illusion and a false belief. Yet here sin is presented as an illusion so powerful and persistent that it is not banished even by the "change called death"!

period will be of longer or shorter duration according to the tenacity of error (p. 77).

We approach death, in other words, with certain errors and sins which have persisted in our lives, despite our best efforts to root them out. After we have "died," these errors and sins are still in our consciousness, so that we must continue to fight against them. The more tenaciously we have held to these errors and sins in life, moreover, the longer will be the duration of this battle. Though on the one hand, therefore, Christian Science minimizes sin by denying its reality, on the other hand sin is, in its teachings, so strong, and the salvation from sin which it offers man is so weak, that man must still fight against sin and error after he has died! This conception of "salvation" is, however, the inevitable consequence of Christian Science's repudiation of the atoning work of Christ. Both here and hereafter such salvation as they teach is wholly by works and not at all by grace!

A "time of probation" after death is therefore absolutely necessary:

> Man's probation after death is the necessity of his immortality; for good dies not and evil is self-destructive, therefore evil must be mortal and self-destroyed. If man should not progress after death, but should remain in error, he would be inevitably self-annihilated.[116]

If man, then, is not successful in this post-mortem warfare against sin and error, he will be self-annihilated. The only conclusion we can draw from the above statement is that this type of individual will eventually cease to exist. Christian Scientists, therefore, in agreement with Seventh-day Adventists and Jehovah's Witnesses, affirm that those in whom error and sin persists shall not be eternally tormented, but shall be annihilated. The teaching that certain people will be annihilated is, however, in flat contradiction to what Mrs. Eddy said about man's having no end, as he had no beginning (p. 338; see above, pp. 40-41).

What happens if man does continue to progress after "the change called death"? "Those upon whom 'the second death hath no power' are those who progress here and hereafter out of evil, their mortal element, and into good that is immortal; thus laying off the material beliefs that war against Spirit. . . ."[117] People who attain this goal arrive at perfection:

[116] *Miscellaneous Writings,* p. 2.
[117] *Ibid.*

> The sin and error which possess us at the instant of death do not cease at that moment, but endure until the death of these errors. To be wholly spiritual, man must be sinless, and he becomes thus only when he reaches perfection (p. 290).

If a person, then, continues to progress after death, continues to grow out of evil and into good, continues to lay aside material beliefs and renounce mortal errors, he will finally reach perfection. Though elsewhere Mrs. Eddy has told us that man is incapable of sin (p. 475), here she proclaims that man has to *become* sinless, and that he can only reach this state of perfection after death, at the end of a long struggle with sin in the hereafter![118]

There is no Hell. As is evident from their teaching on annihilation, Christian Scientists deny that there is a place called hell. Hell, in fact, is defined in the Glossary of *Science and Health* as follows: "Mortal belief; error; lust; remorse; hatred; revenge . . . self-imposed agony; effects of sin; that which 'worketh abomination or maketh a lie' " (p. 588).

> I am asked, "Is there a hell?" Yes, there is a hell for all who persist in breaking the Golden Rule or in disobeying the commandments of God. Physical science has sometimes argued that the internal fires of our earth will eventually consume this planet. Christian Science shows that hidden unpunished sin is this internal fire, — even the fire of a guilty conscience. . . . The advanced psychist knows that this hell is mental, not material, and that the Christian has no part in it.[119]

Hell is here identified with the fire of a guilty conscience, and is said to be mental, not material; thus its distinct existence as a place of punishment is denied. Mrs. Eddy sums up her teaching about hell in a single pithy sentence: "Sin makes its own hell, and goodness its own heaven" (p. 196).

There is no Heaven. If hell as a distinct locality is denied, we would expect that heaven would be repudiated as well. And so it is. Heaven is defined in the Glossary as follows: "Harmony, the reign of Spirit; government by divine Principle; spirituality; bliss; the atmosphere of Soul" (p. 587). Harmony or spirituality, needless to say, do not designate a place; if there is a heaven which a Christian Scientist may enjoy, it must be one which he

---

[118] Note, too, that in all of this discussion about probation after death not a word is said about the saving work of Christ or the help of the Holy Spirit or the grace of God. Surely here is a system of "salvation" from which the last vestige of the gospel of Jesus Christ has been removed!

[119] *The First Church of Christ, Scientist, and Miscellany*, p. 160.

carries along with him. Clear and unambiguous is the following statement: "Heaven is not a locality, but a divine state of Mind in which all the manifestations of Mind are harmonious and immortal, because sin is not there. . ." (p. 291). For Christian Scientists, therefore, both heaven and hell are portable.

There is no Second Coming. At times Mrs. Eddy interprets Biblical references to the Second Coming of Jesus Christ as pointing to the rise of Christian Science: "The second appearing of Jesus is, unquestionably, the spiritual advent of the advancing idea of God, as in Christian Science."[120] In the following quotation this interpretation is made even more explicit:

> It is authentically said that one expositor of Daniel's dates fixed the year 1866 or 1867 for the return of Christ — the return of the spiritual idea to the material earth or antipode of heaven. It is a marked coincidence that those dates were the first two years of my discovery of Christian Science.[121]

This conception of the Second Coming is consistent with Mrs. Eddy's understanding of Jesus as a man who no longer exists, and of Christ as the divine idea which Jesus most fully represented and demonstrated. To affirm, however, that the second appearance of Jesus coincided with the rise of Christian Science is to make Mrs. Eddy equivalent in importance to Jesus Himself. Again we observe a trait typical of the cult: exalting the human leader to equality with, if not superiority to, Jesus Christ.

At another place, however, a Scripture passage referring to the Second Coming of Christ is construed as pointing to a time apparently still future:

> In Colossians (3:4) Paul writes: 'When Christ, who is our life, shall appear [be manifested], then shall ye also appear [be manifested] with him in glory.' When spiritual being is understood in all its perfection, continuity, and might, then shall man be found in God's image (p. 325).

The future tense of the verb "shall be found" in the above quotation indicates that, in this instance, the second appearance of Christ is understood as having not yet occurred. Whichever of the two above-mentioned interpretations of the Second Coming we accept as being the more typical of Christian Science teaching,

---

[120] *Retrospection and Introspection,* p. 70.
[121] *The First Church of Christ, Scientist, and Miscellany,* p. 181. Note that the return of Christ is explained as "the return of the spiritual idea to the material earth." Elsewhere, however, she teaches that there is no material earth.

however, it is quite clear that Christian Scientists categorically deny the literal return to earth of our glorified Saviour at the end of this age.

There will be no Resurrection of the Body. It will be recalled that Christian Scientists deny Christ's resurrection from the dead (above, pp. 47-48). It will also be recalled that the word *resurrection* is defined in the Glossary of *Science and Health* as meaning "spiritualization of thought . . . material belief yielding to spiritual understanding." We are not surprised, therefore, to read on page 291 of *Science and Health*: "No resurrection from the grave awaits Mind or Life, for the grave has no power over either." Nothing is said in the above quotation about a resurrection which might await the body. But since for Christian Science the body does not really exist, it is obvious that there is no room whatever in Christian Science thinking for the doctrine of the resurrection of the body — a doctrine which has been from the very beginning one of the distinctive marks of Christianity.

There will be no Final Judgment. This cardinal teaching of historic Christian eschatology is also repudiated by Christian Science: "No final judgment awaits mortals, for the judgment-day of wisdom comes hourly and continually, even the judgment by which mortal man is divested of all material error" (p. 291).

There will be no New Heaven and New Earth. On pages 572-574 of *Science and Health* Mrs. Eddy gives her interpretation of the passage from Revelation 21 which speaks of the new heaven and the new earth. She affirms that this new heaven and new earth cannot be terrestrial or material, but must be spiritual — at least to the illumined, "scientific" consciousness. This point is made unmistakably clear elsewhere:

> In the Apocalypse it is written: 'And I saw a new heaven and a new earth; for the first heaven and the first earth were passed away; and there was no more sea.' In St. John's vision, heaven and earth stand for spiritual ideas. . . (p. 536).

We have thus seen that Christian Science repudiates every major tenet of Christian eschatology: the teaching that at death one's eternal destiny is irrevocably determined, the existence of hell, the existence of heaven, the Second Coming of Christ, the resurrection of the body, the final judgment, and the new heaven and new earth which will usher in the age to come. As was the case in the other areas of doctrine we have considered, so it is in the area of eschatology: Christian Scientists flatly reject every major doctrine of historic Christianity. Christian Scientists, therefore, have no more right to apply to themselves the title *Christian* than have Buddhists or Hindus — with whose teachings, indeed, Christian Science has greater affinity than with those of Christianity. We conclude that, strictly speaking, Christian Science is neither Christian nor a science.

Bibliography

PRIMARY SOURCES:

Eddy, Mary Baker. *Science and Health with Key to the Scriptures.* Boston: Trustees under the Will of Mary Baker Eddy,[1] 1934 (first pub. in 1875).

————. *Christian Healing.* Boston: Trustees, 1936 (first pub. in 1886).

————. *Christian Science Versus Pantheism.* Boston: Trustees, 1926 (first pub. in 1898).

————. *The First Church of Christ, Scientist, and Miscellany.* Boston: Trustees, 1941 (first pub. in 1913).

————. *Messages to the Mother Church.* Boston: Trustees, 1900, 1901, 1902.

————. *Miscellaneous Writings.* Boston: Trustees, 1924 (first pub. in 1896).

————. *No and Yes.* Boston: Trustees, 1936 (first pub. in 1891).

————. *The People's Idea of God.* Boston: Trustees, 1936 (first pub. in 1886).

————. *Pulpit and Press.* Boston: Trustees, 1923 (first pub. in 1895).

————. *Retrospection and Introspection.* Boston: Trustees, 1920 (first pub. in 1891).

————. *Rudimental Divine Science.* Boston: Trustees, 1936 (first pub. in 1891).

————. *Unity of Good.* Boston: Trustees, 1936 (first pub. in 1887).

————. *Prose Works Other Than Science and Health.* Boston: Trustees, 1925. Contains all of Mrs. Eddy's prose works other than *Science and Health* in one volume.

————. *Manual of the Mother Church.* 89th ed. Boston: Trustees, 1936 (first pub. in 1895).

---

[1] Cited hereafter as Trustees.

CONCORDANCES:

A Complete Concordance to Science and Health. Compiled by Albert F. Conant. Boston: Christian Science Pub. Soc., 1916.

A Complete Concordance to the Writings of Mary Baker Eddy Other Than Science and Health. Compiled by Albert F. Conant. Boston: Trustees, 1934 (first pub. in 1915).

BIOGRAPHIES OF MRS. EDDY:

"OFFICIAL":

Orcutt, Wm. D. *Mary Baker Eddy and her Books.* Boston: Christian Science Pub. Soc., 1950.

Peel, Robert. *Mary Baker Eddy: The Years of Discovery.* N.Y.: Holt, Rinehart, and Winston, 1966.

————. *Mary Baker Eddy: The Years of Trial.* N.Y.: Holt, Rinehart, and Winston, 1971.

The above two volumes are carefully documented and thoroughly researched. A third volume, which will complete this biographical series, is in preparation.

Powell, Lyman P. *Mary Baker Eddy, A Life-size Portrait.* Boston: Christian Science Pub. Soc., 1950 (first pub. in 1930).

Smith, Clifford P. *Historical Sketches from the Life of Mary Baker Eddy and the History of Christian Science.* Boston: Christian Science Pub. Soc., 1941.

Tomlinson, Irving C. *Twelve Years with Mary Baker Eddy.* Recollections and Experiences. Boston: Christian Science Pub. Soc., 1945.

Wilbur, Sibyl. *Life of Mary Baker Eddy.* New York: Concord Pub. Co., 1908. This is *the* approved official Biography.

"NON-OFFICIAL":

Bates, Ernest S., and Dittemore, John W. *Mary Baker Eddy, the Truth and the Tradition.* New York: Knopf, 1932.

Dakin, E. F. *Mrs. Eddy, the Biography of a Virginal Mind.* New York: Scribner. 1930.

Kennedy, Hugh A. Studdert. *Mrs. Eddy: Her Life, Her Work, Her Place in History.* San Francisco: The Farallon Press, 1947.

Milmine, Georgine. *The Life of Mary Baker Eddy and the History of Christian Science.* New York: Doubleday, Page, and Co., 1909.

Springer, Fleta Campbell. *According to the Flesh.* New York: Coward-McCann, 1930.

(Note: Important for the light it sheds on Mrs. Eddy's relationship to Phineas Quimby is Horatio Dresser's *The Quimby Manuscripts.* New York: T. Y. Crowell, 1921; reprinted in 1961 by the Julian Press, N. Y.)

HISTORIES OF CHRISTIAN SCIENCE:
Beasley, Norman. *The Cross and the Crown,* The History of Christian Science. New York: Duell, Sloan, and Pierce, 1952.
————. *The Continuing Spirit.* New York: Duell, Sloan, and Pierce, 1956. History of Christian Science since 1910.
Braden, Charles S. *Christian Science Today*: Power, Policy, Practice. Dallas: Southern Methodist Univ. Press, 1958. History of Christian Science since 1910.
A Century of Christian Science Healing. Boston: Christian Science Pub. Soc., 1966. A history of Christian Science healing during the first hundred years.
Swihart, Altman K. *Since Mrs. Eddy.* New York: Holt, 1931. Dissident movements which have arisen out of Christian Science.

GENERAL WORKS:

BOOKS:

Bellwald, A. M. *Christian Science and the Catholic Faith.* New York: Macmillan, 1922.
Clemens, C. *Awake to a Perfect Day.* New York: Citadel, 1956.
Clemens, Samuel L. (Mark Twain). *Christian Science, with Notes Containing Corrections to Date.* New York: Harper, 1907.
Corey, Arthur. *Personal Introduction to God.* N.Y.: Exposition Press, 1952. An apologetic for the Christian Science way of life, with a sympathetic account of Mrs. Eddy.
Fisher, Herbert A. L. *Our New Religion*: An Examination of Christian Science. New York: Cape and Smith, 1930.
Gillespie, John. *Scriptural References Sustaining the Doctrines of Christian Science.* Boston: Christian Science Pub. Soc., 1901.
Gray, James M. *The Antidote to Christian Science;* or, How to Deal With it from the Bible and Christian Point of View. New York: Revell, 1907.
Haitjema, Th. L. *Christusprediking Tegenover Moderne Gnostiek.* Wageningen: Veenman, 1929.
Haldeman, Isaac M. *Christian Science in the Light of Holy Scripture.* New York: Revell, 1909.
John, De Witt. *The Christian Science Way of Life.* Boston: Christian Science Pub. Soc., 1962. Written by a member of the Christian Science Board of Directors. Contains an account of Christian Science beliefs.
Johnston, Allen W. *The Bible and Christian Science*: A Review of *Science and Health* in Relation to Holy Scripture. New York: Revell, 1924.
Leishman, Thomas L. *Why I am a Christian Scientist.* New York: Nelson, 1958.
Martin, Walter R., and Klann, Norman H. *The Christian Science*

Myth. Rev. ed. Grand Rapids: Zondervan, 1955. History, doctrine, public relations, Christian Science cures.

Moehlmann, Conrad H. *Ordeal by Concordance.* New York: Longmans, Green, 1955. An answer to W. M. Haushalter's *Mrs. Eddy Purloins from Hegel.*

Peabody, F. W. *The Religio-Medical Masquerade:* A Complete Exposure of Christian Science. New York: Revell, 1915.

Peel, Robert. *Christian Science: Its Encounter with American Culture.* New York: Holt, 1958. Written by a Christian Scientist. A study of the relationship between Christian Science and transcendentalism.

Sheldon, Henry C. *Christian Science So-Called:* An Exposition and an Estimate. Cincinnati: Jennings and Graham, 1913.

Snowden, James Henry. *The Truth About Christian Science:* The Founder and the Faith. Philadelphia: Westminster Press, 1920.

Steiger, H. W. *Christian Science and Philosophy.* New York: Philosophical Library, 1948.

Whitney, Adeline D. *The Integrity of Christian Science.* Boston: Houghton-Mifflin, 1900.

Wolcott, P. *What is Christian Science?* New York: Revell, 1896.

PAMPHLETS:

(Note: These are inexpensive, and may be ordered in quantities for distribution.)

Martin, Walter R. *Christian Science.* Grand Rapids: Zondervan, 1957. 32 pp.

Parks, H. J. *Christian Science.* London: Church Book Room Press, 1961. 20 pp.

Talbot, Louis T. *What's Wrong with Christian Science?* Findlay, Ohio: Dunham Pub. Co. 48 pp.

Tanis, Edward J. *What the Sects Teach.* Grand Rapids: Baker, 1958. 89 pp. A brief critical treatment of Christian Science (and of Jehovah's Witnesses, Seventh-day Adventism, and Spiritism).

Wassink, A. *The Bible and Christian Science.* Faith, Prayer, and Tract League; Grand Rapids, Mich. 49504. 19 pp.

Wertheimer, Max. *Why I Left Christian Science.* Findlay, Ohio: Dunham Pub. Co., 1934. 60 pp.

(Note: Some of the above pamphlets can be obtained from Religion Analysis Service, 902 Hennepin Ave., Minneapolis 3, Minn.)